# Dawn Pierce, AD

Assistant Professor of Voice
Ithaca College

Dawn Pierce is an Assistant Professor of Voice at Ithaca College. She earned a master of music in Opera Performance from the University of North Carolina School of the Arts, where she also obtained a postgraduate Professional Artist Certificate (Artist Diploma). In addition, she holds bachelor's degrees in Vocal Performance and Music Education from Ithaca College. Praised as both an exceptional performer and an empowering teacher, she is devoted to promoting a deeper understanding of artistry and self-expression.

Professor Pierce abounds with experience in a wide variety of styles and venues. On the operatic stage, she played Charlotte in *Werther* with Mobile Opera, the title role in *Carmen* with Opera Ithaca, Beatrice in *Beatrice and Benedict* with Asheville Lyric Opera, Olga in *Eugene Onegin* with Opera Carolina and Opera Company of Middlebury, and Madelon and Bersi in *Andrea Chénier* with Nashville Opera. She is equally comfortable in musical theater, where she portrayed Franca in *The Light in the Piazza*, the Grand Duchess in *The Student Prince*, and Anita in *West Side Story*. On the concert stage, she has earned rave reviews for her interpretation of the alto solos in Verdi's *Requiem* and Handel's *Messiah*. She also has been a featured soloist with the Asheville Symphony, the Syracuse Symphony Orchestra, the Warren Philharmonic Orchestra, the Amherst Symphony Orchestra, the York Symphony Orchestra, the Cayuga Chamber Orchestra, the Charleston Symphony, the Binghamton Downtown Singers, the Hamilton College and Community Masterworks Chorale, and the Ithaca College Symphony Orchestra. In addition, she has training in a number of dance styles, stage combat, and opera improvisation.

An innovative recital programmer, Professor Pierce performs frequently in collaboration with great artists such as Charis Dimaras, Emily Newton, and Christopher Zemliauskas. She presented *The Four Types of Love*, a mixed-genre recital exploring the four types of love through song, and was a featured recitalist at the Middlebury Song Fest with her *Wild and Wonderful* American art song program. Her other notable programs include *Written in My Heart*, an interactive recital exploring standard operatic literature in conjunction with technology, fine art, literature, and audience participation; *My Native Land*, a nontraditional solo recital featuring five commissioned works and exploring American genres such as folk, art, opera, musical theater, and spirituals; *The Soprano Sisters*, a humorous narrated program exploring the mezzo-soprano relationship in opera and musical theater; and *Your Opera in a Trunk*, a one-hour improvised opera with plot and characters determined by audience suggestion.

A versatile educator, Professor Pierce has experience as a private teacher, musical director, and master class presenter. In addition to teaching vocal technique, dramatic intention, musical interpretation, and body awareness to undergraduate, graduate, and professional-level singers, she encourages her students to perform frequently and at a wide variety of venues, from professional establishments to local retirement communities.

Not only is Professor Pierce deeply committed to teaching healthy vocal technique, but she is equally invested in both the artistic and personal growth of young artists. For nearly 20 years, she has designed numerous entrepreneurial workshops and programs examining a variety of issues related to artistry and technique. She offers a range of workshops designed to create well-rounded singers at all levels. Example topics include acting, score preparation, fitness, nutrition, mental well-being, effective practice skills, and recital preparation. She has also designed curricula and presented master classes covering audition techniques and improvisation for singers.

# Acknowledgments

Thank you to my teachers:

Penelope Bitzas
Carol McAmis
Elizabeth Mannion
Marilyn Taylor
Ruth Golden
Victoria Livengood
Patrice Pastore
Bill Schumann

# Table of Contents

## Introduction

Professor Biography .................................................. i
Acknowledgments .................................................. iii
Disclaimer .............................................................. vi
Course Scope ........................................................ 1

## Guides

**1**    Anyone Can Sing ................................................ 3
       "Row, Row, Row Your Boat" ........................... 7

**2**    Vocal Warm-Ups ................................................ 8

**3**    Aligning the Spine ............................................. 12
       "Twinkle, Twinkle, Little Star" ....................... 17

**4**    Head and Neck Posture ................................... 18
       "America the Beautiful" ................................ 21

**5**    How to Practice Anything ................................ 23

**6**    The Anatomy and Physiology of Breath ........... 29
       "Happy Birthday" .......................................... 33

**7**    Inhalation for Singing ...................................... 34
       "Rock-a-Bye Baby" ....................................... 39

**8**    Exhalation for Singing ..................................... 40
       "A Canadian Snowfall" ................................. 44

**9**    Coordinating the Phases of Breath ................. 45
       "I Shot an Arrow into the Air" ..................... 50

**10**   Sound Production ............................................ 52
       "Home on the Range" .................................. 56

**11**   Onset: Engaging Balanced Tone ..................... 58
       "Amazing Grace" .......................................... 62

| 12 | Resonance: Exploring Vocal Colors | 64 |
|---|---|---|
|  | "I Softly Sing" | 68 |

| 13 | Utilizing the Soft Palate | 69 |
|---|---|---|
|  | "The Water Is Wide" | 72 |

| 14 | Releasing Jaw Tension | 74 |
|---|---|---|
|  | "Scarborough Fair" | 78 |

| 15 | Your Voice Type | 80 |
|---|---|---|
|  | "Last Rose of Summer" | 86 |

| 16 | Maximizing Your Vocal Range | 102 |
|---|---|---|
|  | "The Star-Spangled Banner" | 108 |

| 17 | Training Your Tongue | 116 |
|---|---|---|
|  | "Ash Grove" | 120 |

| 18 | Articulating Vowels | 122 |
|---|---|---|
|  | "Awake! Awake!" | 129 |

| 19 | Articulating Consonants | 132 |
|---|---|---|
|  | "A Rainy Day" | 137 |

| 20 | Diction for Singing | 138 |
|---|---|---|
|  | "Our Garden" | 144 |

| 21 | Engaging with Lyrics | 147 |
|---|---|---|
|  | "The Alarm Clock" | 152 |

| 22 | Communicating through Song | 154 |
|---|---|---|
|  | "Auld Lang Syne" | 160 |

| 23 | Making Each Performance Personal | 162 |
|---|---|---|
|  | "Danny Boy" | 166 |

| 24 | Singing's Surprising Benefits | 168 |
|---|---|---|
|  | "If Music Be the Food of Love" | 172 |

# Supplementary Material

Glossary . . . 177
Bibliography . . . 181

# Disclaimer

This series of lectures depicts activity that may be considered hazardous or requires unusual levels of physical exertion and should not be undertaken by those without extensive training, practice, and education in the activity, as injury may occur. Please obtain adequate training, practice, and education before undertaking any of the activities depicted. You recognize that there are risks of injury that may occur if you undertake such activity, and you expressly assume such risks and waive, relinquish, and release any claim that you may have against The Teaching Company as a result of any injury incurred in connection with your undertaking the activity. Any undertaking of such activity is done at your own risk. The opinions and positions provided in these lectures reflect the opinions and positions of the relevant lecturer and do not necessarily reflect the opinions or positions of The Teaching Company or its affiliates.

The Teaching Company expressly DISCLAIMS LIABILITY for any DIRECT, INDIRECT, INCIDENTAL, SPECIAL, OR CONSEQUENTIAL DAMAGES OR LOST PROFITS that result directly or indirectly from the use of these lectures. In states that do not allow some or all of the above limitations of liability, liability shall be limited to the greatest extent allowed by law.

# How to Sing

This course invites you to explore both the science and the art of singing. Taught by a professional opera performer and singing teacher with more than 20 years of experience, the course presents a method almost anyone can use to improve their singing skills. This method, rooted in an understanding of the anatomy and physiology of your unique vocal mechanism, provides a solid foundation for steady skills progress and effective artistic expression.

Best of all, these fundamentals of vocal technique can be applied to any style of singing. You don't have to want to be an opera singer to learn from this course. You will benefit from the professor's experience as a teacher, performer, and student. This course distills a lifetime of experience into a practical, effective tool kit that will help you develop awareness of your own vocal mechanism so that you can teach yourself.

It's important to note that this is not a course on how to read music. Reading music is a separate skill and is not necessary for this course. The course materials include both sheet music for those who read music and audio files for those who don't so that you can use your preferred method of learning. As the lessons progress, you should familiarize yourself with the song for each lesson before starting the lesson.

The course begins with an introduction to your respiratory system and the articulatory organs that allow you to make noise as well as the different approaches to learning how to sing. Then, you will learn how to warm up properly for your singing practices and performances.

From there, you will discover the importance of posture to good singing. This is not simply "good posture" that you may have learned as a child; it is an active approach to body alignment that is flexible and responsive to the needs of the moment. This section will explore how not only the spine but also the head, jaw, neck, sternum, and ribcage all affect your singing posture.

Next, you will explore how your posture can support an excellent singing breath. You will learn how singers coordinate the four phases of breath—inhalation, suspension, exhalation, and recovery—to create a habitual breathing pattern that supports your sound.

Then, you will learn about the mechanics of phonation: the actual creation and manipulation of sound. From the muscles around the larynx to the motion of the vocal cords to the shape of the soft palate, you will learn how to shape the resonant spaces of the head and neck to affect the quality of your tone.

No course on singing would be complete without a discussion of vocal range. Are you a soprano, an alto, a tenor, a baritone—or something in between? You will discover how to find your natural range, what you can do to maximize it safely, and how to use this knowledge as a foundation, rather than a straightjacket, when choosing your repertoire.

Next, you will explore the interaction of singing and language. You will study the way the various vowels and consonants of English are formed within the mouth and how to integrate this knowledge with your knowledge of tone to improve your diction.

Finally, once you have studied the mechanics of making sound, you will learn the crucial aspects of performing a song. Whether you want to perform in an opera, a musical, a choir, or a rock band, you will see how to approach each song as a chance for emotional expression and how to make choices that communicate those emotions to others.

By the end of this course, you will have a complete tool kit for understanding how to produce beautiful sound and how to turn that sound into a moving performance for any audience—or even just for yourself.

*For vocal instruction and guided exercises, watch the video lessons.*

# LESSON 1

# *Anyone Can Sing*

*Before starting each lesson in this course, familiarize yourself with the music you'll be singing with the instructor in the video and any materials you might need for the exercises in the video lessons.*

## FEATURED SONG

"Row, Row, Row Your Boat"

## EQUIPMENT NEEDED FOR VIDEO EXERCISES

none

## LIST OF VIDEO EXERCISES

- ❑ **EXERCISE 1**: Sighs and Sirens
- ❑ **EXERCISE 2**: Descending Notes
- ❑ **EXERCISE 3**: Descending Arpeggio

On some level, singing is as natural as crying is to a baby. If you can cry, you can sing. In fact, you don't have to know anything about the voice to sing beautifully. However, you can learn how to make beautiful sounds if you don't already, and you can learn to sing better even if you already feel good about your sound. If you can speak, you can sing.

# From Crying to Singing

What makes a baby cry?

Inside the womb, a fetus gets oxygen from the mother's bloodstream. At that point, the lungs are filled with fluid rather than air. At birth, when you hear a newborn's first cry, what you are actually hearing is the kick-start of the infant lungs. It takes considerable effort to push the fluid out of the lungs and stretch the lungs to be full of oxygen for the first time. Imagine trying to blow up a balloon for the first time; it's difficult to get it started, but then it becomes easier. This is similar to a newborn-lung experience.

How do we move from crying to singing? This course will explore the science of singing as well as the art of singing. Understanding the anatomy and physiology of your unique vocal mechanism provides a foundation for effective artistic expression. A solid vocal technique is to inspired performance as a rich vocabulary is to compelling poetry. In other words, if you want to be a good singer, start with the basics!

Every voice is unique, just like every fingerprint is unique. The combination of your anatomical attributes, genetics, upbringing, and exposure with your unique experiential life story means that every singer has something valuable and special to offer.

Some people don't think they can sing. While there are potentially some inherent physical characteristics that offer advantages to some singers in the same way that height can offer a competitive edge in basketball, singing, like playing basketball, is a skill. Most of the anatomical features involved in singing are highly malleable.

The first records of modern voice teaching date all the way back to the late 1700s. In the beginning, most teachers were empiricists, teachers who derive their teaching from trial and error and observation. By the early 1800s, most recorded methods were utilizing a series of vocalizes with some explanations incorporated.

In 1840, vocal pedagogue Manuel García presented theories on register formation and dissertations on the anatomy and physiology of the vocal mechanism. In 1855, Garcia invented the laryngoscope, which led to the scientific era of singing.

By around 1861, about half the methods in use were empirical and half were scientific. By 1891, almost every new pedagogical idea included sections on anatomy and physiology. But then, around 1896, the idea of the natural voice and attempting to eliminate effort and let vocal reflexes take their course emerged. Pedagogues started to suggest training the mind and the ear rather than just the organs.

Entering the 20th century, approaches to singing seemed to fall out of general agreement. However, there is one thing that most methods agreed on: The physical act of singing is a refined coordination between posture, breath, and tone.

## Methods for Success

There is not one right method for success; there are lots of methods that lead to success. As the singer Ross Halper said, "There is only one way to sing, but there are a million ways to get there."

In this course, because you will not be meeting with a vocal coach in person, you will need to listen carefully to yourself. For this reason, it's recommended that you record yourself singing each time you add a new skill or intention so that you can see how your sound changes. Notice how it feels and how it sounds. In addition to being helpful week to week as you practice, recording yourself singing will also be a wonderful way to measure your progress. If you are diligent in your daily practice, you will get better!

Sometimes the best way to get better at singing involves making crazy noises or doing odd movements. Because you will be working on fine muscle coordination and awareness as you learn how to sing, it is important that you get comfortable making the sounds and doing the exercises in the video. You must be willing to do something you've never done in order to truly transform your singing.

Know that as a singer, you are an athlete. You are a vocal athlete, and your body is your instrument. Just as you wouldn't expect to be able to run a marathon, do a triple axel, or even master a cartwheel in one try, developing your voice takes time and dedication. Singing is the most natural thing we do as human beings; however, improving and refining one's voice takes time and energy.

The goal is for your technique to serve your art. In the beginning, you need to learn and focus on technique, but over time, it will become automatic so that you can simply use technique to serve your message.

## Make Some Noise!

Sighs and siren sounds are tools for freeing the voice. Try the following:

- Take a big breath and let out a little sigh.
- Take a big breath and let out a little bigger sigh.
- Take a bigger breath and go a little higher and lower to make a descending siren sound.
- Try a longer descending siren.
- Try a full siren.
- Try to go lower and higher than before.

You have permission to laugh and have fun in this course. The more freedom and release you find, the better your singing will become.

## Test Your Range

Take a moment to test your range. This will be something fun that you can refer to later. Go as low or as high as you possibly can and just take note of where that is for you.

Write down where your range falls for comparison later in the course (specifically, lesson 16).

It's great to play and experiment with your voice, but be careful about judging your tone. You need to be willing to make some less-than-perfect sounds to gain flexibility and get better.

## How to Get the Most out of This Course

This course utilizes easily accessible and regularly used songs in addition to some special compositions designed just for this course. If you aren't familiar with the common songs, you can consult the supplied audio files. Familiarize yourself with each song before you participate in the lesson. But that being said, focus on making beautiful tone rather than on learning a new song.

This lesson uses a childhood favorite: "Row, Row, Row Your Boat." If you don't know it, familiarize yourself with it and record yourself singing it once just for your information. And keep this recording: It will be fun to refer to it after several weeks of study as a reference point!

Do the vocalizes and exercises featured in the video lessons. Ideally, you'll repeat the exercises for several days in a row before moving on to the next lesson.

Review and return to lessons as often as you like. You may decide to spend several weeks on some lessons. Think of each lesson like a chapter in a book. You are aiming for comprehension despite the fact that there are delineated sections. Over time, you will start to develop your own routine built out of your favorite exercises as you are introduced to new things in every lesson.

> **HOMEWORK**
> Do the vocalizes and exercises presented in the video for this lesson daily. Ideally, you'll repeat the exercises at least five days in row before moving on to the next lesson.

# Row, Row, Row Your Boat

Classic children's song
Music and lyrics accredited to Eliphalet Oram Lyte

Arranged by
Dave Dunbar

© Arranged 2019 for The Great Courses by Dave Dunbar.

# LESSON 2

# Vocal Warm-Ups

**FEATURED SONG**

none

**EQUIPMENT NEEDED FOR VIDEO EXERCISES**

- ☐ yoga mat
- ☐ chair

**LIST OF VIDEO EXERCISES**

- ☐ **EXERCISE 1:** Stretching
- ☐ **EXERCISE 2:** Engaging the Breath
- ☐ **EXERCISE 3:** Hums and Trills
- ☐ **EXERCISE 4:** Sighs and Sirens
- ☐ **EXERCISE 5:** Onset
- ☐ **EXERCISE 6:** Vowel Differentiation
- ☐ **EXERCISE 7:** On Your Head

A warm-up serves to prepare a singer mentally and physically. It gets the blood flowing, muscles moving, breath engaged, and brain ready to make sound. A good warm-up puts the voice in healthy condition, maximizing flexibility, ease, and function. Think of it like the stretching and warming up that athletes do. You *are* an athlete—a singing athlete!

# Warming Up

How do you know when you are warmed up? Well, you just feel it! But there are some specific things to consider to get you started.

Science tells us that after around 10 to 15 minutes of exercise, blood flow increases to muscles, and capillaries open. Body temperature increases, which allows faster muscle contraction and relaxation. Nerve transmission and muscle metabolism are also increased, so muscles work more efficiently.

*The purpose of a warm-up is to build the proper coordination and balance for your most beautiful singing.*

You can use this as a foundational guide and start by taking around 10 to 15 minutes to stretch and warm your mechanism before engaging in your vocal practice. However, you also need to take into consideration that not every day is the same. Many things can affect the readiness of your instrument, such as the weather, the food you eat, the amount of sleep you get, and even your mood. We walk around and live inside our instruments. There will be days when it might take you just a few minutes to warm up and days when it might take you 40 minutes.

So the first step of warming up is to address the state of your instrument.

Have you ever wondered why singers have earned the reputation for always wearing scarves and carrying a beverage? The attempt to maintain the optimum instrument state might have something to do with it.

Think about violinists, who carry their instrument in a case and wax their bows and care for their reeds. Even pianists, who cannot carry their instruments around, carefully manage temperature and humidity for their instrument health.

Likewise, singers need to care for their instruments as well. While a scarf won't guarantee a healthy instrument, pulling a scarf over your mouth to avoid breathing in extremely cold air might help you avoid stiffness or spasms in your lungs. Lungs warm and humidify air as you inhale. This warming and humidification starts in the mouth and nose. The air you inhale will achieve 100 percent humidity and be warmed to body temperature long before it gets deep into the lungs.

In that process, the cool air you inhale will cool the lung tissue a little, but when you exhale, you're exhaling warmed air that adds some heat back to those tissues on its way out. This explains why you can see your breath when the air temperature is cold. Wearing a scarf that can be pulled over your mouth can help prewarm the air before you breathe it.

What about the water bottle or cup of tea? Many singers swear by honey-and-lemon water or tea to keep their vocal cords healthy. This is somewhat of a myth—fluid never touches your cords. However, even though it doesn't touch your cords directly, being hydrated is certainly critical to vocal health.

Adequate oral hydration, by drinking noncaffeinated drinks, keeps your cords healthy and your mucus lubricating. Your vocal cords are small and delicate and move hundreds of times per second. Just like lubricating machines allows for maximum efficiency, ease, and wear, keeping your vocal cords flexible, hydrated, and lubricated is critical. But note that it takes around four hours for the fluid you drink to have an effect on your vocal cords, so think ahead!

Before you even start your official daily warm-up, recognize that you are carrying your instrument with you everywhere you go. Every decision you make about caring for your body will affect your vocal mechanism. When you realize that your health affects your singing so directly, being a singer can help guide you to make better decisions about caring for your body. Between the need to stay hydrated, rested, and energized and the constant massage that your internal organs get while singing, singing can have significant health benefits for you.

## Physical Warm-Ups

Start every practice session with a physical warm-up and a vocal warm-up. In fact, starting with a physical warm-up might make your vocal warm-up take less time. You can be creative and find your own ways to wake up and energize your body, but here are a few ideas about how to engage physically and awaken your instrument before intense activity:

o Go for a walk.

o Get on an elliptical.

o Go for a quick jog or run.

# Vocal Warm-Ups

Be very intentional while warming up your voice, but avoid judging the voice during your warm-up. Warming up is exactly the right time to make less-than-beautiful sounds in service of building flexibility and strength.

Start making sounds using a closed mouth, such as hums or trills. Explore different sounds, going over any spots in the voice that you feel a hitch or any lack of ease. Here are a few examples to play with:

- A lip-tongue trill, otherwise known as blowing a raspberry, involves taking a deep breath, sticking your tongue out, and blowing with a consistent breath to make a noise. Next, try it with pitch! If you enjoy this, do it throughout your vocal range. If this isn't for you, keep playing with it for now and try some other trills that you might like better.

- A tongue trill, or alveolar trill, is a sound produced with your tongue. You place the tongue at the alveolar ridge, found between the upper teeth and the hard palate. Say "butter" slowly and pause on the middle consonant. Notice that you are closing off air at the back and sides of your mouth while tapping the alveolar ridge. Next, say "butter" fast, in repetition. Go back and forth between saying "butter" fast and then move into a tongue trill. Keep playing with it! Then, add pitch.

- To do a lip trill, or lip bubble, pretend you are really cold and say "brrrr." You can put pressure on the corners of your mouth with your fingers to help relax your lips if you are having trouble. You are looking for the least amount of tension: release your shoulders, neck, and jaw and use a balanced and steady breath. Then, try it with pitch.

You might find one or more of these trills to be natural, or you might find them all illusive. Continue to play with all of them in your vocal study. They are learned skills, and you can develop the flexibility and coordination to create these sounds over time. If you are struggling with the trills, you can keep playing with them or switch to using a hum.

You might be surprised by how much better your voice will feel after just a few exercises! New exercises will continue to be introduced throughout this course; you can find all of them in the video lessons. If you want more variety or deeper exploration, there are many vocalize books that are filled with fun and engaging exercises. Feel free to also invent your own exercises as you gain confidence and knowledge. Be creative and learn to trust your instrument.

*The lessons in this course have been designed to follow your warm-up, so before you start each lesson, take a few moments to get your instrument ready to engage!*

# LESSON 3

# *Aligning the Spine*

## FEATURED SONG

"Twinkle, Twinkle, Little Star"

## EQUIPMENT NEEDED FOR VIDEO EXERCISES

- ❑ foam roller
- ❑ yoga mat
- ❑ chair or weight bench/piano bench
- ❑ five-pound weights or water bottles or cans of food

## LIST OF VIDEO EXERCISES

- ❑ **EXERCISE 1**: Finding Your Neutral Spine Position
- ❑ **EXERCISE 2**: The Pelvic Clock
- ❑ **EXERCISE 3**: Thoracic Stretches
- ❑ **EXERCISE 4**: Bent-Over Row
- ❑ **EXERCISE 5**: The Garcia Position

One of the most amazing things about being a singer is that you are your own instrument! Your instrument functions like no other in that it is a dynamic, living thing. In order for you to make the most of your instrument, you need to engage your body in creating the most advantageous space for your music making to take place. In the world of singing, this is often referred to as having good posture. Posture is a living, breathing place of existing; it is not a static, locked position.

# The Anatomy of Posture

A flexible alignment is the foundation upon which to build a solid vocal technique.*
To start, you need to analyze your specific body and current strengths and challenges. Take a photo of the front and side of your body to start your analysis. You might even take a moment to record a video of yourself singing this lesson's song, "Twinkle, Twinkle, Little Star,"† so that you can measure your progress throughout this lesson.

Next, look at the pictures you took and note your alignment. Draw lines on your photos, both from the side and from the front, to notice any patterns. Some common things you might notice from the side are a forward head position or an exaggerated sway backward. From the front, you may notice an elevated shoulder, a tilted head, or imbalanced hips.

Remember that you are working with an instrument that is alive and dynamic. Posture is more than just a snapshot in time, so don't worry if you are imbalanced.

Close your eyes and take notice internally of your alignment, avoiding judgement. Think about what you learned from your photo. Does it align with your experience internally?

*Think of* posture *as an action verb—an active and buoyant idea rather than a specific position or static place. It is continually changing and moving with every breath and thought.*

Next, sing "Twinkle, Twinkle, Little Star" and see if anything changes. You may even want to record yourself now to see if anything postural shifts as you sing, or even as you think about singing.

Then, watch your video. Did you notice anything? Sometimes just thinking about singing can encourage an exaggeration or shift in posture.

Now that you have an idea about what your current neutral alignment looks and feels like, you can explore ideas on how to develop the best version of your personal alignment for singing.

The spine provides the foundation from which all human movement originates, and developing an understanding of a

---

\*    Claudia Friedlander's *Complete Vocal Fitness* offers detailed tools for assessing your dynamic alignment.

†    If you prefer to sing the alphabet song or "Baa, Baa, Black Sheep" to this tune, feel free! All of these songs are sung to a variant of the 1761 French melody "Ah, vous dirai-je, Maman," a popular melody utilized and arranged by many composers over the years, including Mozart's famous variations.

well-aligned, dynamic spine is crucial to developing a solid vocal technique. The spine is the foundational structure that supports all of the moving parts that are used for singing. The spine facilitates breathing as well as activities of the larynx, articulators, and resonators. This foundational structure is extremely mobile.

The spinal column consists of 24 vertebrae, plus the sacrum and the coccyx. Starting at the head, the first seven vertebra are described as the cervical spine, the middle 12 are the thoracic spine, and the last five before the sacrum are called the lumbar spine.

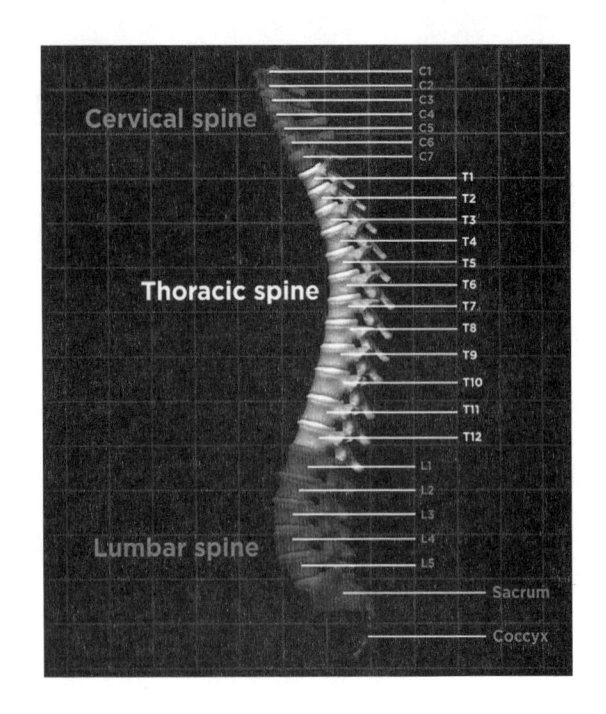

## Finding a Neutral Spine Position

For singing, you are looking for a neutral spine position that includes all of the natural curves of the spine. A great alignment tool that's used to assess a neutral spine position is a foam roller. You want to have one that fits at least the length of your torso. The video exercises for this lesson will help you find your optimal dynamic posture to facilitate your best sound production.

The small bump at the base of the skull, called the occipital bun, or inion, and your sacrum are parallel. With the awareness that the inion and sacrum are generally in the same plane, you can create a dynamic range of motion that will optimize the range of motion for your larynx and articulators in the cervical spine. You can also find the maximum range of motion in your ribs and diaphragm through the thoracic and lumbar spine.

In your search for a neutral spine, some common things to watch for are a protruding forward head posture and a forward pelvis tilt. When your pelvis is tilted forward, you will experience tightness in the back and weakness in the abdominal muscles.

Good lower body alignment facilitates a full range of motion for the diaphragm and ribs and provides a shell for core stabilization. Hopefully, you can feel that the breath is three-dimensional when the body is in better alignment, allowing for full range of motion.‡

---

‡ David and Kaethe Zemach-Bersin and Mark Reese's *Relaxercise* includes many exercises to help you work on finding your best dynamic posture.

Having good posture is important in that it allows you to get a deep, full breath. If you are collapsed, your diaphragm can lock and not move freely. The breath and posture should work together. Remember to resist the temptation to place yourself in a specific position but rather work to encourage balance and efficiency as you build strength and awareness.

*Singing is a full-body activity. Your body is your instrument!*

## Elevating the Sternum

Often in our society, with computers and smartphones and driving, we find our sternum dropped and our chest muscles very tight. This will limit your capacity to take a full breath. Imagine that there is a hook under your sternum holding you up. A slightly elevated sternum can be helpful for breathing related to singing; however, it is critical that the elevation of the sternum happens holistically.

It is a balancing of the thorax that helps to maintain an open and flexible feeling. Be careful not to arch your body in an effort to elevate the sternum. Instead, find a more expansive and flexible thorax while maintaining ease and length in the lower spine.

There are some stretches and strengthening exercises you can do while working to find your version of a slightly elevated sternum, avoiding a collapse or depression. These stretches and exercises, several of which you can find in the video lesson, will also have the potential benefits of improving your overall posture.

In addition to stretching the potentially tight muscles in the front of your body, you also want to balance this by strengthening the back and shoulder muscles. You can do strength exercises to engage in a better posture in general, helping you maintain the elevated sternum you want for singing. Maintaining the elevated posture in singing will also improve your posture in daily life, so it's a win-win relationship.

Over time, you will build the strength and stamina to keep your sternum high. While this can seem daunting if this is an area of challenge for you, you can completely transform your posture by strengthening your back and stretching your front.

# Working on Your Posture

As far back as the early 19th century, singers have been working on their posture. Manuel García, one of the most prominent voice teachers and pedagogues of the bel canto era, encouraged practicing with hands crossed behind your back and palms outward in the lower back area while singing. This is now referred to as the Garcia position. Remember that as you are working to coordinate a beautiful singing posture, your alignment should always be dynamic and never locked, even while engaging in the Garcia position.

Beginners may be bothered by slight backaches while learning to sing and breathe. This is common but shouldn't be of concern—in fact, it is a sign of success! Your muscles are gaining elasticity and strength. Don't ignore the discomfort; treat it like you would any muscle ache (stretch, apply ice or heat, etc.). As you gain strength and coordination, the aches should subsist. If not, see a medical professional.

Once you reach the end of the video lesson, record and photograph your posture. See if you note any change in assessing your alignment after doing the video exercises. Then, sing "Twinkle, Twinkle, Little Star," taking another video as you engage with a more buoyant posture. What do you notice?

---

**HOMEWORK**

Imagine the progress you'll make if you continue to engage in this lesson's exercises and others to find your optimal dynamic posture. Repeat the exercises in the video lesson daily for at least three weeks and then pick your favorites to continue regularly as a part of your daily practice.

# Twinkle, Twinkle, Little Star

Traditional nursery rhyme/lullaby  Arranged by Dave & Peg Dunbar

LESSON 3—ALIGNING THE SPINE

♪ = 120

*mf*

A, B, C, D, E, F, G, H, I, J, K, L, M, N, O, P, Q, R, S, T, U, V,

Doub-le U, X and Y and Z. Now I know my A, B, Cs. Next time won't you sing with me!

Twink-le, twink-le lit-tle star. How I won-der what you are, up a-bove the world so high,

like a diam-ond in the sky. Twink-le, twink-le lit-tle star, how I won-der what you are.

Baa, baa, black sheep, have you an-y wool? Yes, sir! Yes, sir! Three bags full. One for the Mas-ter, and one for the Dame, and

one for the lit-tle boy who lives down the lane. Baa, baa, black sheep, have you an-y wool? Yes, sir! Yes, sir! Three bags full!

© Arranged 2019 for The Great Courses by Dave & Peg Dunbar.

# LESSON 4

# Head and Neck Posture

## FEATURED SONG

"America the Beautiful"

## EQUIPMENT NEEDED FOR VIDEO EXERCISES

- ❏ chair
- ❏ foam roller

## LIST OF VIDEO EXERCISES

- ❏ **EXERCISE 1**: Finding Neutral Head and Neck Position
- ❏ **EXERCISE 2**: Maintaining Neutral: Lying Down
- ❏ **EXERCISE 3**: Maintaining Neutral: At the Wall
- ❏ **EXERCISE 4**: Maintaining Neutral: Standing

In the previous lesson, you worked on maintaining the height of the sternum, and this lesson focuses on head position. These two things go together. When you drop your sternum, you tend to naturally shift your head forward. When you lift and open your sternum, your head position naturally wants to be taller and more buoyant. This lesson explores head and neck postures that support a freely functioning vocal mechanism.

*Posture is a dynamic, ever-changing balance shift. It is not a set position but an alive and energetic engagement in coordinating your physical attributes.*

## The Cervical Spine

Your neck is made up of seven cervical vertebrae that have flexibility, allowing for lots of movement in this area.

Start by sitting in a chair so that you can focus on your cervical spine. Put your hand on the back of your head. Start at the top and move slowly toward the base of the skull. Feel for a bump at the back of your head. This is your inion, or the occipital bun. It sits at the base of the skull and is the part of the occipital bone that protrudes from the back of your head. This is essentially where the top of your spine is.

To truly get a feel for where this is in relation to your vertical plane, put your fingers gently in your ears and nod your head back and forth. Take a moment to look in the mirror while touching these points.

Note that this is the level of your atlanto-occipital joint, where the top of the spine meets the head. Starting at the skull base, your head connects to C1, your top vertebrae, also called the atlas.* Beneath the atlas lie the rest of the vertebrae composing your cervical spine. Most people can feel C7 most prominently at the base of the neck.

Head position is very important for singing. The larynx, or voice box, is housed in your neck, roughly in the position between C3 to C6. Your vocal cords are inside the larynx.

Finding balance in the head and neck is crucial to ease in vibration. You must use the dynamic posture of your head and neck in the service of sound production. The posture of the head and neck affects the positioning and balance of the internal vocal mechanism, especially in regards to laryngeal and supraglottal vocal tract function. A well-aligned spine facilitates access to free laryngeal movement.

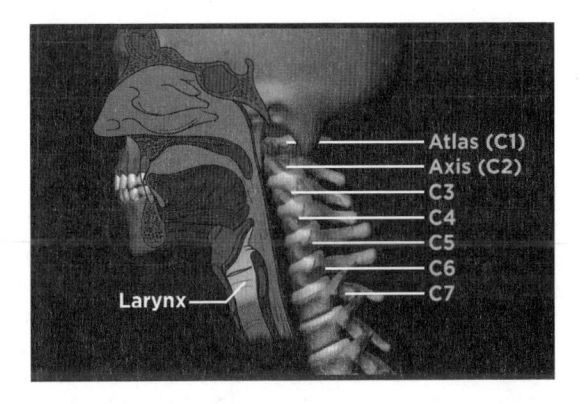

---

\*   This vertebra is named for Greek mythology's Atlas—who was condemned to hold aloft the celestial globe—because it supports the globe of the head, which is the skull.

# Finding Your Optimum Dynamic Posture

Singing is intensely affected by your head posture. With so much flexibility in the cervical spine, you want to be sure to choose your dynamic posture with an understanding that some movements encourage ease in phonation and others do not. Start paying attention to this in your daily practice. Even a slight shift in position can change your experience.

The head being out of alignment increases the weight and pressure on your neck and upper back muscles significantly. The actual weight of your head is up to 13 pounds. If your head is balancing forward and up from the top of the spine, it produces a lengthening and stretch in the body, offering a lightness and ease. Finding this balance is not only good for your singing but also for your daily comfort.

Today, one of the most common posture challenges for singers is the chicken position. Due to the electronic devices we use, we tend to constantly be engaged with our heads shifted forward. Aside from being less than ideal for vocal function, this also leads to strain in the neck and back and can cause headaches and pain. This forward head position also leads to vocal fatigue over time, whether singing or just speaking.

When singing, you might be tempted to shift out of your optimum dynamic posture as you inhale or as you move to a high note. Some of this is mental, and some of it is physical. When you reach your head forward, it might feel like you can get air, but you don't need to shift your head forward to do so.

In some ways, shifting your head forward into the chicken position can make it easier to hit a high note. It does elongate the cords in a sense. It pulls your muscles out of their natural positions and causes strain in the muscles surrounding the larynx as well as the vocal cords themselves. But it isn't sustainable over time. Like a rubber band that is constantly pulled and held tight, over time your cords will suffer and fatigue, losing their buoyancy. This position also won't create the most beautiful tone or the most comfortable sound production.

You want your body to function with the greatest efficiency and ease. Engaging in a balanced posture is critical for singing—and life.

When thinking about posture, imagine a string holding you up from the top of your spine, like a puppet. Play with this imagery while singing this lesson's song, "America the Beautiful." Engage your posture continually and actively while singing. Check in and feel your tall, lengthened, light spine. Incorporate the images from both posture lessons with an open sternum, naturally curved spine, and floating head. Record a video of yourself if you aren't sure whether you are where you want to be and note any progress or areas for continued improvement.

Know that it takes time to build flexibility and strength if these postures are not already natural for you. Be patient and kind to yourself in the process. A well-aligned spine creates a strong foundation on which to build your solid singing technique. Continue to pay attention to your posture throughout your journey to beautiful singing.

# America the Beautiful

Music by Samuel A. Ward
Lyrics by Katherine L. Bates

Arranged by
Dave & Peg Dunbar

© Arranged 2019 for The Great Courses by Dave & Peg Dunbar.

"America the Beautiful"  [page 2]

# LESSON 5

# How to Practice Anything

**FEATURED SONG**

none

**EQUIPMENT NEEDED FOR VIDEO EXERCISES**

none

**LIST OF VIDEO EXERCISES**

none

Regular practice is crucial to improving your singing skills, and developing your voice takes time and dedication. In order to practice effectively, you'll need to find a space that you feel comfortable making noise—not just one that you feel you can sing beautifully in, but one that you can make some terrible and silly sounds in as well. You'll also need to set aside around 30 minutes a day for practicing. As your vocal mechanism develops and stamina increases, you can add more if you like. Effective, efficient practice involves three main skills: evaluating, strategizing, and integrating.

# Evaluate

When evaluating your singing progress, you should focus on your short-term goals and individual lessons to determine whether you are achieving. Avoid getting distracted by the goal of sounding a certain way. Imagine that you are building your voice in a similar way that you build a house. You need to dig and build the foundation, wire for electric, install plumbing, etc., before you can choose the perfect paint colors and accessories. So, when you are evaluating your success, be sure that you are focusing on your current goals.

You should also get specific, as each lesson in this course will guide you to focus on specific skills that will improve your singing. While singing is a very natural and holistic art, breaking it down and focusing on specific elements will help you identify where you might need work and therefore should spend your focused time and attention.

You are strongly encouraged to record a video of yourself if possible. This is because one of the hardest parts about being a singer is that you will likely never be able to truly hear yourself. The sound you hear in your head is very different than what is being heard by other people.

Have you ever heard your speaking voice on a recording and thought that you didn't sound like yourself? The truth is that you really do sound like that—or at least the recording you hear is much closer to what others experience when they hear your voice.

Why do you experience your voice so differently than everyone else does? To start, how do we hear in general?

Sound waves enter through the outer ear via air conduction and travel through a narrow passageway called the ear canal, which leads to the eardrum. The eardrum vibrates from the incoming sound waves and sends vibrations to bones in the middle ear for amplification. The vibration then moves to the inner ear to a structure called the cochlea, a snail-shaped structure filled with fluid. The waves move tiny hair cells that eventually create an electrical signal that is carried by the auditory nerve to the brain.

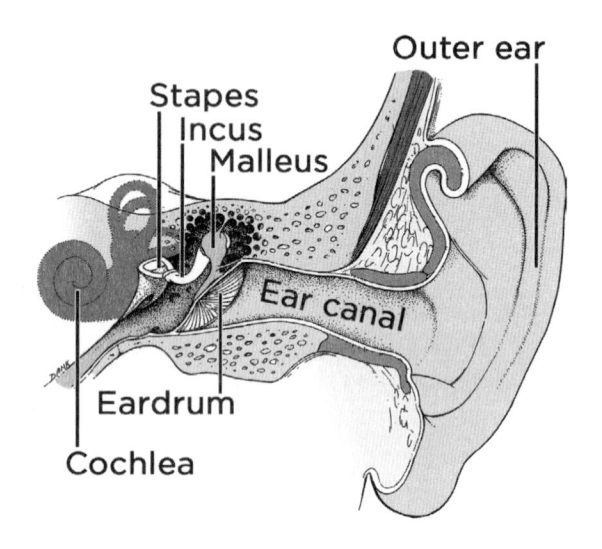

When you sing or speak, not only are you hearing via the air-conducted pathway, but you are also experiencing a bone-conducted pathway of sound. The bones and tissue in your head conduct their own sound waves directly to the cochlea in the inner ear. These structures tend to enhance the deeper, lower-frequency vibrations, because when they travel through the bone, they spread out and lower in pitch.

The voice you hear in your head includes both pathways. When you hear your voice on a recording, you are only experiencing the air-conducted sound. Often, the sound you hear on a recording sounds higher or thinner than what you are accustomed to hearing because it is void of the bone-conducted sound waves you are accustomed to hearing.

If you record yourself regularly, you can learn to associate the feeling and sound of your voice internally with the tone that others are experiencing when they hear you. Despite the fact that it will always sound different in your head than what you hear on a recording, you can grow more comfortable with your external sound.

Another way to explore the sounds you are capable of is to put in earplugs. If you do this, you can experience your voice isolating the bone-conducted vibrations.

Not only will you never hear your own true voice—even with advances in technology—but there are so many things that affect the way you perceive a sound, including overtones, undertones, acoustic space, etc., that your voice will even sound different in different spaces and rooms.

However, recording yourself will give you a better idea of how you sound than your internal experience. It is good to develop a relationship between what you hear on a recording and the feeling that you are experiencing while creating sound.

When you listen to your recordings, listen for changes in tone quality. Does your tone sound breathy or clear? Bright or dark? Balanced or strident? Also, listen to intonation. How is your pitch? Flat, sharp, or just right? Most importantly, listen for how things sound in relation to how they felt. Often, a tone that feels better to you also sounds better in general, and that relationship is critical to trusting and developing a solid vocal technique.

## Strategize

After you have heard the things you need to work on, the next step is to develop a careful method, or plan of action. This is the main thing this course will help you do. Big-picture ideas about how things function will be presented, and you will be given specific exercises for addressing them. As you move through the course, you will gain confidence in utilizing the strategies presented to evoke positive change in your singing.

Be creative in expanding the exercises you try in the video lessons. Be playful and use the ideas, concepts, and exercises as a foundation to jump-start your practice. Once you feel you've mastered one of the exercises, take it to the next step. Do you have a song that you love to sing along with on the radio, a favorite childhood song, or a song you have always wanted to learn? You can apply the strategies offered in this course to any music—any sound—and it counts as practice. When it comes to vocal development, what you are singing is not nearly as important as how you are singing it.

# Integrate

Finally, you integrate your newfound skills.

Coordination is built with slow and deliberate repetition. Think back to when you learned to read a book, ride a bike, or drive a car. First, you established the essential skills. Then, you had to practice and repeat until you increased your confidence and improved your coordination and speed.

Have you ever noticed that a child asks to read a book over and over again or wants to play the same game again and again? Repetition provides the practice that you need to master new skills. Repetition strengthens the connections in the brain that help you learn.

Why is repetition so important?

Our brains have two kinds of neural tissue: gray matter and white matter. Gray matter processes information, directing and signaling our nerves, while white matter, which is mostly made up of fatty tissue and nerves, improves the speed and transmission of nerve signals. To sing, information has to travel to the white tissue. The axons of white matter are wrapped in a fatty substance called myelin, which seems to change with repetition.

Science has discovered that it's well-established neural pathways that create habits. Think of it like a path that evolves in the woods. The first time you wander on a hike and end up at a beautiful waterfall, you didn't follow a path. The next time you try to find the waterfall, you may or may not find it, but as you keep trying and eventually establish your route, the path will become clear in the ground. Eventually, you won't have to think about it; you'll be able to make your way to the waterfall easily by following the well-established path.

The goal is that the singing work you do will eventually become habitual so that you don't have to work so hard to do it. While singing, you want to be able to direct your brain to intention and communication rather than on technical creation of sound.

In the beginning, you may have to think about your posture, breath, phonation, articulation, etc., when singing, but eventually, these new skills will be integrated and become habit. Like any change you make, in the beginning it might require careful attention, but as the neural pathways are clearly established, the process becomes faster and more efficient. Your singing will improve over time.

Studies have found that in order to integrate new information, you should work in short, regular sessions. In the beginning, you should practice in 15- to 30-minute sessions once or twice a day. It is important that you maintain regular, focused practice sessions and don't try to put all your work into one day.

Once the pathways have been physically established, it is possible to reinforce what you've learned by imagining it. But it isn't enough to *only* think about the exercises. While mental practice can be very effective, you actually have to engage in creating those neural pathways to eventually reap the benefits of mental practice. Just as you can't just read a recipe and expect to have dinner on the table, you'll have to follow the instruction and engage with the video exercises to create your technique in support of your own unique voice.

## A Typical Practice Session

Here is what a typical practice session should look like:

- First, warm up. Remember, some days it will take 2 minutes whereas other days it might take 25. Starting your vocal warm-up with a physical warm-up might make your warm-up time shorter. Don't count this as practicing; this is readying yourself for practice. Use your warm-up lesson again and again until you feel confident and comfortable warming yourself up. You don't need to record your warm-up; let it be free of judgement and more about finding the feeling of readiness to sing.

- Next, work on assigned vocalizes and/or exercises that are challenging you while you are freshly warm vocally and your brain is rested and ready for a challenge. This is a great time to record yourself in little spurts so that you can compare what you are physically experiencing with what sound is being created in the space you're in.

- Then, apply these skills to your music. As your skills develop and you start to tackle more difficult repertoire, divide your music into sections. You don't want to always start at the beginning of a piece. For optimal efficiency, start with a section that is challenging you and apply the technical skills you are working on to make it feel better. Develop those myelin-insulated pathways for the section. Repeat it successfully several times. Make sure the pathway you want to follow is well established.

- Finally, integrate the challenging section into the full piece. Think of this like a reward for your hard work.

*Reading music is great when you are learning something long or complicated that is difficult to remember, but it won't be necessary for this course. Learning by ear is faster and easier in general.*

*If you already have music-reading skills or if you want to work separately on reading music while you're still learning to sing, scores are provided for the music used in this course.*

# Learning New Music

Learning new music, including establishing the notes and rhythms for a new piece, doesn't necessarily count as vocal practice. But it can if you are thinking about how you are singing.

So often when we are learning notes and rhythms, that is all we are thinking about. Once those tunes are learned, we can add another level of thought and intention.

At this point in your practice, you can learn notes and rhythms for new pieces. It is fun to challenge yourself to learn a new piece every week or every month.

You will now apply all of your practice skills, implementing everything you've learned in the first few lessons, to a new piece. This is how you will want to proceed throughout the course—building skill and repertoire throughout. You don't need to only practice the piece you are learning or working on in the lesson; you can practice anything you've learned in the course, even in sequentially later lessons if you're skipping around. The important thing is to apply the skills and techniques you are learning to whatever you are singing.

Sometimes it is critical to just sing for fun, without thinking about these technical ideas. Just like you aren't always practicing for giving a public lecture when you speak, you don't always have to be practicing for a performance to sing.

You can't focus on everything you want to happen vocally at one time. Instead, break it down. Take the time to focus on elements of your technique in every song, piece by piece. It will all come together.

Now apply all you've learned about posture and good practice habits as you continue your journey to better singing.

# LESSON 6

# The Anatomy and Physiology of Breath

**FEATURED SONG**

"Happy Birthday"

**EQUIPMENT NEEDED FOR VIDEO EXERCISES**

- ❏ chair

**LIST OF VIDEO EXERCISES**

- ❏ **EXERCISE 1**: Back Stretch
- ❏ **EXERCISE 2**: I'm a Little Teapot
- ❏ **EXERCISE 3**: Complete Exhale
- ❏ **EXERCISE 4**: Five-Count Hiss
- ❏ **EXERCISE 5**: Exhale without Collapse
- ❏ **EXERCISE 6**: Exhale on Trill

Singing strengthens the lungs, and the opposite is also true: Building strength and flexibility of the lungs is critical for improving your singing. This lesson explores the respiratory system, a foundational element for your vocal progress. You'll learn about the organs and structures that come into play when you sing, and you'll be introduced to exercises that increase the flexibility and improve the function of your breathing. These exercises will have both immediate and long-term benefits for your singing.

> *"Singing is like a celebration of oxygen."*
> – Björk

# The Anatomy of the Respiratory System

The respiratory system is a series of organs responsible for taking in oxygen and expelling carbon monoxide—in other words, inhaling and exhaling. There are three major parts to the respiratory system: the airway, which includes the mouth, nose, pharynx, larynx, trachea, and bronchi; the lungs; and the muscles of respiration, including the intercostal muscles and the diaphragm. The airway functions to warm, moisturize, and filter the air before it enters the lungs.

The pharynx is comprised of the space behind your mouth. You can gently touch the front outer wall of your larynx, often referred to as an Adam's apple.* The trachea lies below the larynx and runs down behind the sternum, or breastbone, and is about four inches long. It then divides into smaller tubes called bronchi that get smaller and smaller and eventually lead into the lungs.

The lungs are made of a spongy material that attaches to the ribs by the fluid-filled pleural sacs. Surely you know how important the lungs are to breathing. But what can be surprising is exactly how big they are and where they are specifically located.

Find your clavicle,† or collarbone. It's the long bone that you can feel at the top of your torso, just below the neck. The upper border of your lungs is way up under your clavicle. Now find the bottom of your rib cage. There are seven ribs that are attached to the cartilage on the breastbone, or sternum, and then there are some floating ribs. Find the place where you can let your fingers reach up and inward a bit. This is where the bottom of your lungs are. Next, trace along the bottom edge, following it around to the back, and that is the lower border of your lungs. Your lungs are slightly bigger in the back and actually lie closer to the back than to the front.

---

\* Men tend to have more prominent Adam's apples than women, but women do in fact have them as well.

† The clavicle is the only long bone that runs horizontally in the body!

The third major part of the respiratory system are the muscles of respiration, including the intercostals and the diaphragm. The intercostals are the muscles between your ribs that work on your inhale and exhale, because they open and close. The three layers of intercostals coordinate to expand and contract the rib cage: The external intercostals assist in inhalation by pulling on the ribs and helping to expand the lung cavity, while the internal intercostals and the innermost intercostals help in exhalation.

The other muscle of respiration is the diaphragm. When the lungs expand, your organs get displaced—more specifically, the diaphragm moves down and pushes them out. When you traced the bottom of your rib cage, you basically touched your diaphragm.

The diaphragm is the main muscle of respiration. It is a thin, dome-shaped layer of muscle and tendon that separates the abdominal cavity from the chest cavity. It is horizontal and essentially divides your body in half from top to bottom.

The diaphragm attaches at the intercostals, along the lower rib cage, behind the front of the sternum, and in the back lower spine. The diaphragm also attaches to itself by a central tendon, making the diaphragm one of the most unique muscles in the body. The diaphragm uses its central tendon and its attachments as leverage to flatten during inhalation. The diaphragm is active on inhalation; it is used to pull air in, not to push air out (like an upside-down plunger).

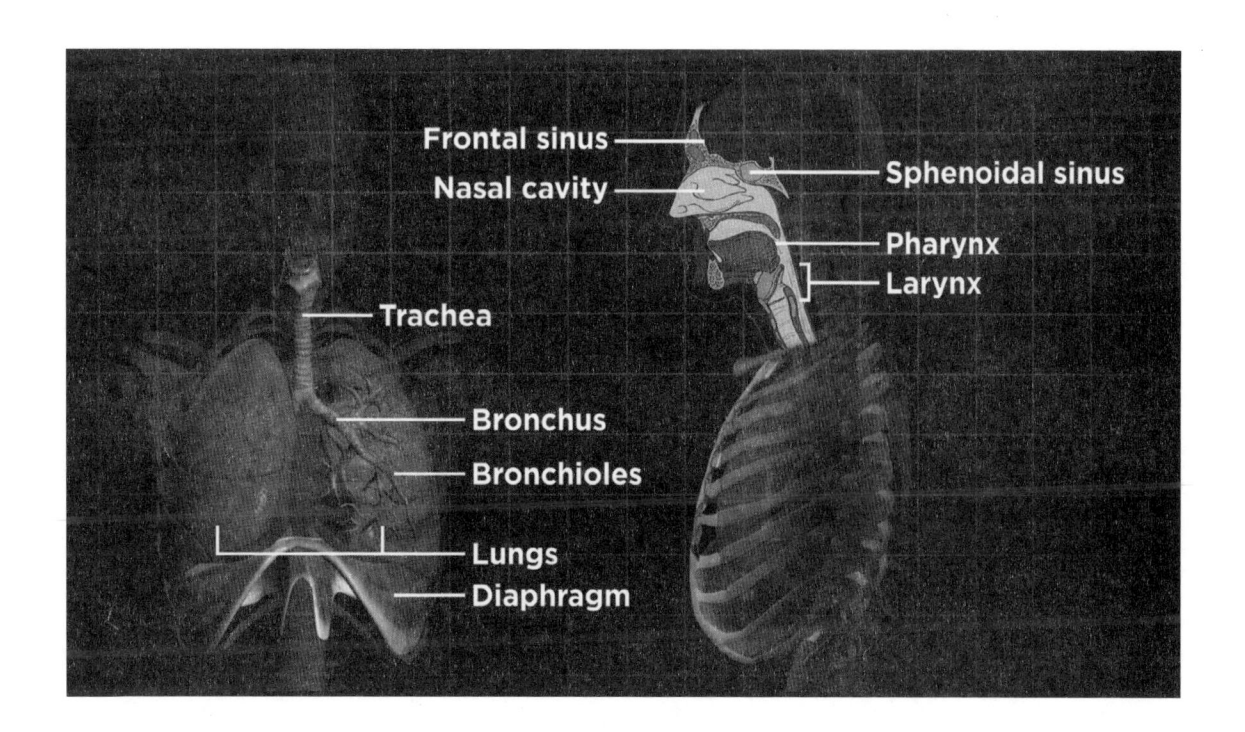

# Breathing like a Singer

Although singing is natural, there are some obstacles. One big challenge is that although the diaphragm is the primary muscle of respiration—and breathing is the foundation of good singing—we can't control the diaphragm. In other words, we can't control the thing that controls singing!

The diaphragm is incapable of providing sensation. Our conscious mind has no direct control over it. In order to get the diaphragm to cooperate, it needs help from the sternum and the intercostals. Basically, we trick the diaphragm into doing its job by not allowing the sternum or the rib cage to collapse so quickly.

The video exercises in this lesson work on increasing your awareness, flexibility, and lung capacity. Note that an ideal inhalation for singing allows breath to enter the nose and the mouth at the same time. This allows for maximum release.

Science will tell you that inhalation is active. However, singing is going to tell you that you need to think of the inhalation as passive. Imagine your body wanting to be full of air as the diaphragm does its job. Allow the exhale to be the active part of the breath while the inhale is passive—a release.

Sing this lesson's song, "Happy Birthday," once and record yourself so that you can review it later and note your progress. Then, after working on this lesson's video exercises, sing it again, applying everything you learn about breathing.

---

**HOMEWORK**

Practice every day this week, repeating the exercises you learned in the video lesson until they begin to feel easier. Over time, the flexibility and directionality of your breath will become more natural. You can also integrate this lesson's video exercises into your everyday practice routine. They will give you a great foundation for creating beautiful sounds as well as potentially lift your energy and mood.

# Happy Birthday

Music and lyrics attributed to
Patty & Mildred Hall

Arranged by
Dave & Peg Dunbar

*Lyrics:* Happy birthday to you! Happy birthday to you! Happy birthday, happy birthday! Happy birthday to you!

© Arranged 2019 for The Great Courses by Dave & Peg Dunbar.

# LESSON 7

# *Inhalation for Singing*

## FEATURED SONG

"Rock-a-Bye Baby"

## EQUIPMENT NEEDED FOR VIDEO EXERCISES

- ❏ foam roller or yoga mat or blanket

## LIST OF VIDEO EXERCISES

- ❏ **EXERCISE 1**: Breathe like a Baby
- ❏ **EXERCISE 2**: Three-Part Breath Lying Down
- ❏ **EXERCISE 3**: Three-Part Breath Standing
- ❏ **EXERCISE 4**: Three-Part Breath with Sigh
- ❏ **EXERCISE 5**: Isolating the Breathing Muscles

While inhaling is natural, breathing for singing requires some attention. While science will tell you that the inhalation part of breathing is active, in singing you need to imagine that the inhalation is passive. The ideal breath for singing will be taken through the nose and mouth together for a free, noiseless inhalation.

## Common Breath Issues

Some of the most common breath issues are developed with good intentions. For example, some people breathe high and shallow in an effort to breathe fast and be accurate with how much time the music allows for a breath. Other people breathe loudly in an effort to signal to their pianist when they are going to sing. Still others stack their inhalation in an effort to not run out of breath too soon.

Maybe most commonly, people barely breathe at all because they are so afraid to move their shoulders and chest; they've been told that it's bad to have a high breath, so they become fearful of taking an expansive breath.

While all of these habits were formed in earnest, they can be released as ideals.

---

*For most babies and young children, their entire bodies visibly respond to every breath.*

---

## Finding a Calm, Tension-Free Breath

Grab a foam roller, yoga mat, or blanket and prepare to relax. Lie down. Get comfortable. Find that place you go when you are very relaxed, just before you go to sleep.

Close your eyes. Take a moment to slow down and bring attention to your breath—without judgement. Just scan for information. Imagine the calm, released breath you find when you have crawled into bed after a long day.

Do a body scan. Start by bringing attention to the center of your body. Imagine a warm drop of water falling into your belly button and follow the warm rippling slowly throughout the body.

Start by noticing the movement in your abdomen as your stomach rises and falls. Do you notice that the movement is three-dimensional? Can you feel your back and sides moving as well? Notice the intercostals between the rib cage expanding and contracting. Notice the chest rising and falling.

Are you aware of any movement at the pelvic floor? Don't force anything; just allow yourself to notice your breath.

Keep expanding your attention to the wider ripple. Can you feel any movement in your buttocks or thighs resulting from your breath? How about in your chest or shoulders or scapula area?

Continue to expand your awareness. Bring your awareness up into the neck, front and back, and down to your knees. Allow the ripple to take you into your head and move down past your calves into your ankles and feet. Observe the sensations you are experiencing throughout your body while breathing in and out.

If your mind begins to wander during this exercise, just notice. Without judgement, bring your mind back to focus on what you are feeling. Observe and experience the shifting and changing movement in the body from moment to moment.

If you find yourself holding tension, feel free to soften and release on the next exhalation. Can you expand your awareness all the way to the face, the back and top of the head, down the arms to the fingertips, and down to the tips of the toes? Feel the gentle rhythm of the breath as it moves through the body.

Sit up slowly. What did you experience?

Remember that when you inhale, the diaphragm contracts, moving downward and increasing the amount of space inside your chest cavity. Your lungs expand into this space. Meanwhile, the intercostal muscles, which are between your ribs, are also helping to expand the chest cavity by contracting and pulling your rib cage up and out.

Your expanding lungs suck air in through your nose or your mouth—or both. That air travels down your trachea, or windpipe, which splits into two bronchial tubes, which lead to your lungs. Inside the lung, the air finally reaches the alveoli: the air sacs where oxygen can enter your bloodstream and carbon dioxide can leave it. Then, on the exhale, everything happens in reverse. Your diaphragm and intercostals relax, pushing the air back up into your mouth and nasal cavities.

Now return to your relaxed position, just noticing how things might be the same or different when you sing this lesson's song, "Rock-a-Bye Baby." Sing it slowly, phrase by phrase, taking plenty of time between phrases. Does your inhalation change? Can you maintain the holistic connection to the full body? Is any part of you holding out or engaging differently? Can you make a different choice? Just play with it.

Don't worry too much about how you sound or what is happening as you are exhaling. Focus on the inhalation part of the process.

Finally, slowly come to standing and break down what you experienced. Where did you feel your inhalation? Did anything change when you sang?

*We can all find more freedom and flexibility in our breath.*

# Types of Breath

There are three main types of breath most humans engage in: clavicular, thoracic, and diaphragmatic.

Clavicular breathing involves breathing just into your upper chest. Take a few breaths in and out and see how this feels. On the next breath, filling only this upper-chest chamber, sing the first phrase or two of "Rock-a-Bye Baby." You can allow your sternum to press down on the singing so that when you release for the inhale, you'll likely return to the clavicular breath. Note how this feels and sounds. This high, shallow breathing is not ideal for singing—or, frankly, for life.

Thoracic breath is a more expansive breath, focusing on the rib cage. Allow your rib cage to collapse as you exhale. Do your best to isolate this part of the breath. Try this while singing the first few phrases of the lullaby again. The breath is going into the ribs—into the intercostals. This is likely better than clavicular breathing, but it's not ideal for singing. While we want our rib cage to expand as we breathe, only breathing in the ribs is incomplete.

Now release into the low, diaphragmatic breathing you learned about in the previous lesson. For now, attempt to isolate this as well. Exhale from the bottom, blowing it all out, and then release. The breath goes down, into the diaphragm. Try it with a few phrases of the lullaby. With diaphragmatic breathing, you are getting closer to the ideal. However, you want the most expansive and released breath possible for singing. Ideally, you utilize all parts of the breath in one!

In yoga practice, pranayama is the formal practice of controlling the breath. Most, if not all, yoga practices work with a three-part breath that correlates nicely with the clavicular, thoracic, and diaphragmatic breath areas. With the three-part breath, you fill first the belly, then the rib cage, and finally the upper chest. Then, you exhale in reverse.

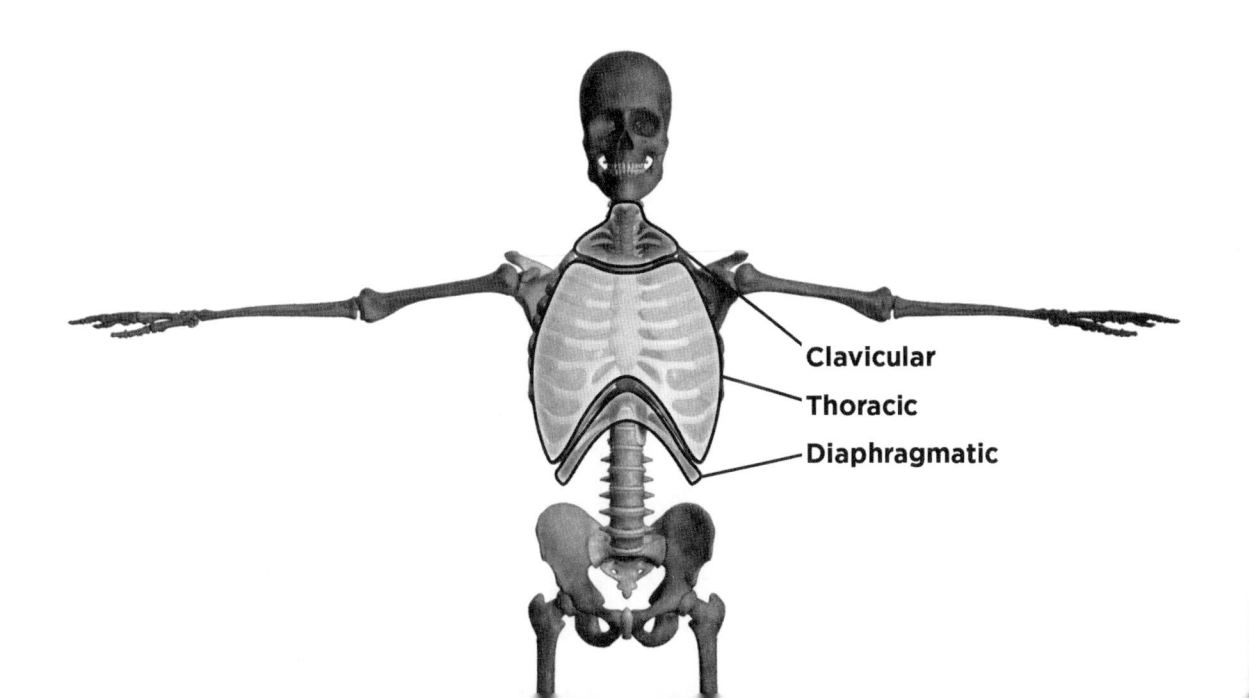

Remember the work you did on posture. Having the sternum up will assist with engaging diaphragmatic breathing. If you allow your sternum to collapse, then it will "recover" by going back up, encouraging a directionality of up rather than down for the inhalation.

Remember that the diaphragm is an inactive muscle, yet we need to engage it in order to vacuum in our inhalation. So rather than avoiding a high breath, you are opening and expanding your space before the inhalation so that your breath is naturally low and expansive.

A successful diaphragmatic breath is the kind of breath you want to employ for healthy singing. It is probably the one you should use in daily life, too—it's the healthiest one for many reasons. One reason this is important is because singers often need to take quick "catch breaths"; it's not always possible to take as much time as you'd like in a song to breathe.

Remember that posture is dynamic and moving and buoyant, rather than a locked position. Having good posture allows you to get a deep, full breath. If you are collapsed, your diaphragm can lock and not move freely. The breath and posture should work together.

Rediscovering an expansive and released inhalation is crucial to creating a healthy sound. Continue to apply these concepts to all of your songs and vocalizes. Over time, you'll grow more confident and comfortable in applying these techniques to your singing.

# Rock-a-Bye Baby

Traditional nursery rhyme/lullaby  
Arranged by Dave & Peg Dunbar

Rock-a-Bye baby on the tree-tops. When the wind blows, the cradle will rock. When the bough breaks, the cradle will fall, and down will come baby, cradle and all. Yes, down will come baby cradle and all.

© Arranged 2019 for The Great Courses by Dave & Peg Dunbar.

# LESSON 8

# Exhalation for Singing

### FEATURED SONG

"A Canadian Snowfall"

### EQUIPMENT NEEDED FOR VIDEO EXERCISES

- ☐ coffee sipping/stirring straw or normal straw
- ☐ glass filled halfway with water

### LIST OF VIDEO EXERCISES

- ☐ **EXERCISE 1**: Sternum Lift
- ☐ **EXERCISE 2**: Attempting Appoggio
- ☐ **EXERCISE 3**: Maintaining Appoggio: Hung-A
- ☐ **EXERCISE 4**: Maintaining Appoggio: Hiss
- ☐ **EXERCISE 5**: Maintaining Appoggio: Dog Pant
- ☐ **EXERCISE 6**: Maintaining Appoggio: Trill
- ☐ **EXERCISE 7**: Straw Siren
- ☐ **EXERCISE 8**: Blowing Bubbles
- ☐ **EXERCISE 9**: Trill on Song

Studies have shown a strong association between anxiety and shortness of breath. It is a result of the fight-or-flight response. This is a reflexive response, so we can automatically go into panic mode when we are feeling out of breath. But being at the end of your breath in singing can be a good thing. If you are at the end of a breath, then you have had a good exhalation. Then, when you release for the inhalation, you'll get a deeper inhalation. The quality of the exhale determines the quality of the inhale.

# Different Ways to Exhale in Singing

Stand tall. Inhale and then exhale normally without any resistance.

This time, inhale and exhale on a relaxed hiss, allowing everything to collapse.

Now try exhaling and pushing the low belly out. This is a method of breathing called the *Bauchaussenstütz* technique, or belly breathing. This is a different kind of resistance than is being encouraged in this lesson. Notice that when you push the low belly out, you are more likely to collapse the sternum and rib cage.

Now do it the opposite way: Inhale and hiss while leaning your body out, against its desire to go in, as you exhale. Keep it all out for as long as you can. Anticipate that the rib cage and torso are going to want to collapse and lean against it. Allow the low belly to be neutral rather than push out. This is working toward the technique of appoggio. Repeat this several times.

If you are having trouble coordinating this directionality, stop for a moment and see if you can simply flex your intercostals out without any breath involved. This is the direction you want to allow as you exhale in this version of the breath.

Now try another hiss.

Notice that in the appoggio technique, the sternum and pectoral muscles remain relatively stationary, without induced rising or falling. The rib cage stays generally expanded near the position of inspiration. There is no pressing down in appoggio. You want to avoid the excessive outward tension.

Note that you are leaning against anything that wants to collapse, including the sternum and the rib cage. Keep the sternum up; you want to feel full and open.

You're going to have to fight against the collapse. When you can't take it anymore, you can release and inhale again. Repeat this. In the beginning, it might feel like a lot of work, but once you get used to it, the breath can feel free and easy in this direction, too.

Now try it with this lesson's song, the original composition "A Canadian Snowfall." To compare and feel the extreme, sing all the way to the end of the breath. Aim for getting through the whole piece in one breath—just for fun. It's OK if you don't make it all the way to the end of a phrase.

The first time through, allow your sternum and rib cage to collapse as you sing "A Canadian Snowfall" as far as you can in one breath.

Next, try it using appoggio. Try to sing it all in one breath again. Everything is going to want to collapse, and you're going to fight against it. Repeat the intention with as much dynamic energy as you can muster. It isn't stiff; it is fluid and energized.

Now go phrase by phrase utilizing the technique of appoggio. Release the inhalation and resist the collapse. You might not be able to keep your sternum high and ribs expanded while singing right away, but you can practice it and it will get better.

Many times, people feel a lot of tension when they start to apply the appoggio technique. While the long-term goal is to feel ease and release, there is some tension in singing. There can't be action—specifically, the creation of sound—if there's not some sort of friction and dynamic movement. There should be a push and a pull.

What we do in singing is try to control where the tension is; we want to keep it away from the phonating mechanism. When using the diaphragm, and controlling the air, we're trying to get all the tension in the mechanism down below the diaphragm.

You want to keep tension off the vocal cords, which are small and thin.* Below them, you've got the whole body, with all kinds of muscles that support your vocal mechanism. Embracing and enhancing these elements of your mechanism will strengthen your singing, creating ease, flexibility, and stamina.

By suspending the collapse of the sternum and rib cage, you are taking a big step in developing your technique as a singer. Some singers describe this as feeling like you continue inhaling even as you exhale. During the bel canto era, the Italian school of vocal technique called this type of breathing appoggio,† which can be defined in this context as "to lean against the desire to collapse."‡ So rather than simply inhaling and exhaling with the normal cycle (usually around four seconds: one in, three out), you use some intention in your exhale, slowing the return of the diaphragm.

## Straw Phonation

One technical exercise that has blossomed over the past decade is the use of straw phonation, which helps you balance and focus your exhalation.

Find a straw. Women will be best served by a straw that has a tiny diameter, like a coffee sipping/stirring straw. Men can use a traditional straw. Avoid the large smoothie straws; they don't quite have the same effect. The smaller the straw, the more challenging the exercise, so play around to find your perfect size for this lesson and perhaps aim for something smaller as you get more proficient.

Put the straw in your mouth and make sound. Be sure you aren't letting air escape around the straw or through the nose.

---

\*     The vocal cords are two bands of elastic muscle tissue that are approximately somewhere between the diameter of a dime and a quarter, depending on your gender and voice type.

†     To be clear, appoggio is not only related to the exhale. It is a term encompassing the complete system of balanced support, including not only the muscles of respiration but also the muscles of the larynx and their intrinsic and external framework.

‡     The translation of *appoggio* from Italian is "to lean" or "to support."

Straw phonation is sometimes compared to doing aerobics in the water—there is less impact and stress on the vocal cords. It has a similar effect as the trills. Vocal scientists called it a semi-occluded vocal tract exercise. When the mouth is partially closed, back pressure reflects at the lips to help the folds vibrate with more ease and less muscular effort in the mechanism.

Take your straw and do a siren. Go as low and high as you feel comfortable.

Now that you've played once, remember to employ your appoggio technique. Does it make a difference in how high and low you can go or how much energy and power is in your sound? Repeat this several times.

Next, sing the tune of "A Canadian Snowfall" with the straw. Inhale through your nose and straw, releasing the breath but engaging in your dynamic posture.

Have you started to notice that even if you are successful in engaging in an open feeling at the beginning of a phrase, as you start to run out of breath, it is harder to resist the collapse? This is completely normal. Just keep engaging low rather than letting it creep up.

Celebrate when you are at the end of the breath and don't panic! Remember, if you are at the end of a breath, then you have had a good exhalation. When you release after a complete exhalation, you'll get a deeper inhalation.

Here's another straw exercise: Get a glass and fill it halfway with water. (Use a half glass or you'll likely get a bit of a shower!) Put your straw into the water and gently blow some bubbles. Next, see if you can do a siren while blowing bubbles up and down while keeping the size of the bubbles consistent. This shows you that you have a consistent airflow.

When you feel comfortable with that, try it with the "A Canadian Snowfall" tune while keeping those bubbles bubbling.

# HOMEWORK

Practice every day this week, repeating the exercises in the video lesson.

# A Canadian Snowfall

Lyrics based on a poem by
Rosanna Eleanor Leprohon

Music by
Dave & Peg Dunbar

*Lyrics:*

Come to the case-ment, we'll watch the snow soft-ly des-cend-ing on earth be-low,
fair-er and whit-er than spot-less down, or the pearls that gleam in a mon-arch's crown,
cloth-ing the earth in its robe's bright flow; is it not love-ly, the pure white snow. Yes,
is it not love-ly, the pure white snow.

© Written 2019 for The Great Courses by Dave & Peg Dunbar.

# LESSON 9

# Coordinating the Phases of Breath

**FEATURED SONG**

"I Shot an Arrow into the Air"

**EQUIPMENT NEEDED FOR VIDEO EXERCISES**

- ❏ exercise band or abdominal support band
- ❏ foam roller or yoga mat
- ❏ book
- ❏ chair
- ❏ 2 full grocery bags or suitcases

**LIST OF VIDEO EXERCISES**

- ❏ **EXERCISE 1:** Farinelli Maneuver Variations
- ❏ **EXERCISE 2:** Breathe against Resistance
- ❏ **EXERCISE 3:** Breathing on the Floor
- ❏ **EXERCISE 4:** Cat/Cow
- ❏ **EXERCISE 5:** Slow, Single-Nostril Breathing
- ❏ **EXERCISE 6:** Sternum Lift with Weight
- ❏ **EXERCISE 7:** Heavy Object Hold
- ❏ **EXERCISE 8:** Crossed Limbs

Some people think about breath in two phases whereas others think about breath in four phases. But either way, the coordination of the phases of breath is crucial. This lesson breaks down breathing into four phases associated with singing: inhalation, suspension, exhalation, and recovery. You'll explore and coordinate these phases, working toward creating habitual patterns for breath.

## The Physics of Breath

We have this false idea that lots of breath comes through our mouths when we sing. However, the physics of breath tells us that once the breath hits the vocal cords, it is transformed into vibration and is no longer air. These are sound waves.

Place a mirror, or even just your palm, around 12 inches away from your face and make vowel sounds (any vowel will work, but most consonants won't). A clean tone production should produce less condensation/breath flow. This is a fun way to explore how you are utilizing your tone at this point.

*Modern voice research has produced an instrument called an electroglottograph that displays percentages of breath emission in tone.*

## The Breath Cycle

This exercise consists of the four breath-cycle segments: inhalation, suspension, exhalation, and recovery. You'll start with four counts in each of the first three steps and gradually add one count each time. Play with this daily and see if you can increase your ease and capacity. Over time, gradually increase the count on each cycle, with a long-term goal of 12 counts.

Don't look for more air as you increase the count; instead, pace your breath differently each time. In healthy singing, you never want to feel crowded or stuffed with air. When you are in the suspension part of the exercise, be certain not to engage in any tension or grabbing in the vocal cords. Keep all your energy low.

Now see how far you can get!

- Inhale for four counts.
- Suspend in the inspiratory position for four counts.
- Exhale over four counts without sound.
- Immediately repeat step one.
- Continue (eventually through a count of 12).

Remember to do your best to engage in your best expression of posture. Your posture will inform your breath in significant ways.

Now try the same exercise with this lesson's song: "I Shot an Arrow into the Air."

Note that phrases can be divided in many ways. As a singer, it is part of your preparatory process to determine where in the music you will breathe. This is an artistic and technical decision. You should think about the text, the punctuation, the musical line, and your technical facility. Try a few different ways with the first section of the song, each with a different configuration of phrase length. The slashes indicate the end of the phrase and thus where you breathe.

> I shot an arrow/
> into the air/
> It fell to the earth/
> I knew not where/
> For so swiftly it flew/
> that my sight could not follow it/
> in its flight/

How did that feel? What are some other choices you could make?

Next, try this with longer phrases overall. Note that when you add tone, you are looking for efficiency in your breath. Try the following phrasing:

> I shot an arrow into the air/
> It fell to the earth I knew not where/
> For so swiftly it flew that my sight could not follow it in its flight/

Did that feel easier or harder? Perhaps surprisingly, singing a longer phrase often feels easier. Remember, the quality of the exhale determines the quality of the inhale. If you are getting rid of more breath, it is likely that your inhalation will be more expansive and released, setting you up for a more supported tone in the following phrase.

Now go through the whole piece with this in mind. Determine where you would like to breathe. You can use some combination of the previous options or divide the song in any way that feels artistic and fun to you.

You can use the "suspend" part of singing if you would like to honor punctuation without moving into another part of the breath cycle. This can be important when you want to avoid stacking the breath, which is a feeling of old breath remaining in the lungs while a new breath is taken in for the next phrase. The result is a stacking breath pressure, which throws off the balance and ease in tone creation.

Thinking about appoggio and allowing the breath to release from the bottom up can help this. It's like a tube of toothpaste: It is much easier to use all the toothpaste if you squeeze from the bottom. If you collapse, or squeeze, the top, it is harder to access the stale air, or trapped toothpaste.

Try this so that you can recognize what to avoid when you are planning your breath when approaching new pieces. Take a good breath and sing the first line of "I Shot an Arrow into the Air," but this time, inhale before every word.

How did that feel? Not great, right?

Now return to your favorite version from your previous exploration of phrasing. Pay attention to all parts of the process—from inhalation, to suspension, to exhalation, to recovery. Try engaging the abdominal muscles up and in before you take your first breath. This gives a similar feeling to being at the end of the breath and getting a good inhalation. It encourages a deep release, allowing the diaphragm to lower and the lungs to expand, engaging a complete inhalation. Now sing "I Shot an Arrow into the Air."

How did that feel? Did you like your choices?

Next are some tools to troubleshoot based on your own individual needs. Feel free to try these, but perhaps integrate the ones that feel the most relevant to you into your regular practice routine.

If you are finding it difficult to stay expanded on your exhalation, try adding resistance to build strength and awareness. You can use an exercise band or abdominal support band. Secure the band around your rib cage, keeping your sternum high. Then, engage in hiss, tone, or this lesson's song.

If you are finding it problematic to allow the abdominals to naturally engage up and in rather than pushing out when you sing, lie on your back on a mat or foam roller or directly on the floor. Place a book on your stomach. When you inhale, allow the book to rise up. As you exhale or engage in tone, allow the book to settle toward the floor.

If you are finding trouble tapping into the feeling and flexibility of the back expanding, try the cat/cow yoga pose, in which you gently flow between two poses, giving a nice stretch to the spine

## Troubleshooting Tools

and encouraging your breath to be low and deep.

If you are having trouble slowing your breath and finding awareness, try this nostril-breath exercise. Sit up tall in a chair. First, take your right pointer finger and cover your right nostril gently so that no air comes in through it. Breathe in deeply through the left nostril. Then, switch to covering the left nostril with your finger while you exhale through the right. Reverse and repeat this several times. Constricting a nostril forces you to slow down your breathing. Take note of the release on the inhale as you expand and the gentle inward motion of the stomach as you exhale. Even in this exercise, imagine that you are continuing to expand during the exhale in the upper body.*

Are you still having trouble keeping the sternum up while singing? This can take time. Return to the posture lessons and continue to do your strength training with back and shoulders and stretching the muscles of the sternum to find more length and pliability. In addition, there are

---

\* Imagine that you are a hot-air balloon and that the diaphragm is the opening of the balloon. As you exhale, you are pulling the fire into the balloon. Be sure to keep the base of the balloon expanded to reap the benefits.

a few exercises you can do to work on the muscular engagement that you want lower in your body in order to free the upper body and find ease.

- Try holding a heavy item, such as a grocery bag filled with groceries or a filled suitcase, in each of your hands while singing. Use your singing posture in the upper body and lift with the legs. Take one heavy object in your left hand and another in your right. Lift the objects and breathe while lifting. Hopefully, you will find it difficult to lift your shoulders or collapse the sternum while holding these objects.

- Another exercise to get some dynamic engagement in the lower body without collapsing the sternum involves a balance board, a tool commonly used to improve core strength in the exercise world, while singing. Because you have to continually balance as you sing, you are much less likely to be still.

Keep in mind that you can work on the breath any time—while you are walking to work, cooking dinner, working on the computer, driving, or exercising.

---

*This is the last lesson that will be specifically dedicated to studying the breath for singing, but keep in mind that every sound you make while singing is informed by the breath. Whether you are a beginner or an advanced singer, you should continue to work on awareness and intentionality in your breathing. Feel free to refer to these breath lessons and exercises at any point in the process.*

# I Shot an Arrow into the Air

Lyrics based on "The Arrow and the Song" by
Henry Wadsworth Longfellow

Music by
Dave Dunbar

"I Shot an Arrow into the Air"   [page 2]

# LESSON 10
# Sound Production

### FEATURED SONG

"Home on the Range"

### EQUIPMENT NEEDED FOR VIDEO EXERCISES

☐ Drinking straw

### LIST OF VIDEO EXERCISES

☐ **EXERCISE 1**: Zzzzz...
☐ **EXERCISE 2**: Glottal Attack
☐ **EXERCISE 3**: Sirens
☐ **EXERCISE 4**: Siren with Straw
☐ **EXERCISE 5**: "Gah-Geh"
☐ **EXERCISE 6**: Self-Massage

Your vocal cords, or vocal folds, on their own sound like an unintelligible buzzing tone. This is called phonation—the process of generating raw vocal tone. It is how we describe the vibratory action of the vocal folds, which is where we control pitch and create tone.

# The Anatomy of the Larynx

Find your larynx, or voice box.* It is located in front of your cervical spine at the level of the third, fourth, fifth, and sixth vertebrae. Put your hand gently on the front of your throat and swallow. When you swallow, you can feel the hyoid bone† hinge upward. The larynx is suspended from this independent bone. As you can feel, the larynx is very mobile—partly because of this flexible attachment.

The cartilage, ligaments, and muscles of the larynx function together in an intricate process to house and support the vocal folds. At the top end of the larynx is the epiglottis: a flap that essentially guides food to enter your stomach rather than your airways and vocal cords. It basically keeps you from choking.

At the other end of the larynx is the cricoid cartilage, which forms a complete ring around the trachea. It provides the foundation for the muscles and ligaments aiding in sound creation and breath passage. There is a flexible ligament connecting it to the trachea, continuing the important flexible nature of the laryngeal anatomy.

Sitting on top of the cricoid cartilage is a pair of pyramid-shaped cartilages called the arytenoid cartilages. Between them is the thyroid cartilage. This is the largest piece of the larynx. Most people can feel the thyroid cartilage on the front of their larynx by putting their hand gently at the front of their neck. It's the Adam's apple.

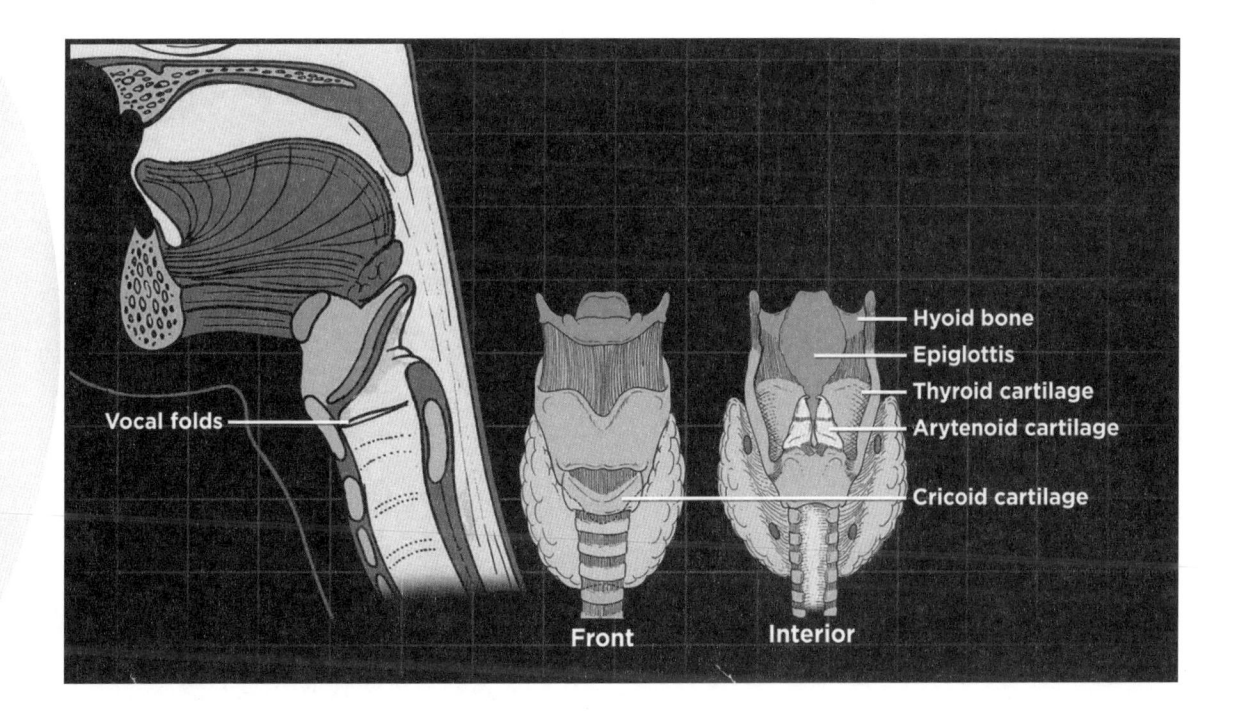

---

\*      This is a pretty accurate description since your vocal cords are inside the larynx.

†      The hyoid is the only bone in your body that isn't attached to another bone.

> Why do we refer to the thyroid cartilage as the Adam's apple?
>
> *It is related to story of the forbidden fruit with Adam and Eve from the book of Genesis in the Hebrew Bible. In the story, when Adam ate the forbidden fruit, some of it was lodged in his throat. He and his descendants were cursed to keep the chunk of fruit to make sure no one ever forgot this sin.*

Generally, all people start out with thyroid cartilage of the same size, and it grows during puberty. Larger larynxes are more prominent and can be seen and felt more easily in the front of the neck/throat. Men tend to have a more pronounced laryngeal prominence because their larynx tends to be larger.

There are many ligaments, membranes, and muscles that control the laryngeal movement. The extrinsic muscles, or muscles outside the larynx, support and stabilize a fixed laryngeal position. The intrinsic muscles, or muscles inside the larynx, are largely responsible for sound production.

## The Vocal Folds and Pitch Control

Your vocal folds are made up of twin infoldings of tissue stretched horizontally from back to front inside your larynx. They are attached in the front to the thyroid cartilage and at the back to the arytenoid cartilage. They vibrate, modulating the flow of air being expelled from the lungs during phonation. This space is open during inhalation, closed when the breath is being held, and apart a tiny bit for sound production. This is also called the glottis, which refers to the folds and the space between the folds. The length and width of your vocal folds are one significant determinant of your voice type. Generally, the larger the larynx, the longer the cords and the lower the voice.

How is pitch made through these folds? The folds vibrate when they are forced open by increased air pressure in the lungs; they close again as the air rushes past the folds, lowering the pressure. In other words, a negative pressure is created between the vocal folds that sucks them toward each other. This is called the Bernoulli principle.

> Did you that know your vocal folds are white?
>
> *They are white because of the minimal blood circulation.*

It is the same principle that makes the wings of an airplane lift.

The Bernoulli principle is key to healthy vocal production. The right amount of airflow allows the folds to vacuum together with just the right amount of effort, without squeezing or too much muscular effort.

The direction of your breath is bottom-up. The vocal cords act like wind instrument reeds in that they vibrate up and down. So, air travels up from your lungs and meets the underside of the vocal folds and causes them to vibrate. The number of times these folds vibrate per second is what controls pitch.

## Exploring Your Phonation

When you are singing, you want to try to maintain a balanced, generally low laryngeal position. Laryngeal stability relies on balance and coordination rather than control. The challenge is that there are many muscles that elevate and depress the larynx. You are looking to stabilize the larynx with a dynamic equilibrium.

You want the larynx to feel at ease, so you need to avoid lifting the larynx by avoiding tensing the muscles that potentially lift and tighten. One muscle that tends to pull at the larynx is the digastric muscle, which attaches the hyoid bone to the jaw in the front and the skull in the back.

While laryngeal stability is a source of contention among voice teachers, most instructors agree that excessive raising or lowering of the larynx impedes free vibration—but a general feeling of stability is ideal. However, attempting to keep it still or in a specific place will result in undesired tension.

Imagine that you have a string pulling from the center of the top of your head toward the ceiling. While engaging in this active posture, massage under your jawline, starting back by the ear and moving toward the chin. Repeat this several times until you feel a supple and easy reaction.

Next, using your fingers, move to the back of the head. Massage the muscles right next to the spine just below the head. While massaging this area, tilt your chin toward your chest and then return to neutral. Repeat this several times.

Then, while massaging the muscles just below the head at the back of the neck, sing this lesson's song: "Home on the Range." Can you encourage your neck to remain supple and released while singing? Don't press, but you can use your hands to feel how much or how little you are engaging in external tensions. Vibration and movement are good, but reduce and remove any extraneous tensions, especially in the laryngeal area, while still engaging with your energized breath.

## HOMEWORK

Work on the video exercises every day this week.

# Home on the Range

Music by Daniel E. Kelley
Lyrics by Dr. Brewster M. Higley

Arranged by
Dave & Peg Dunbar

Oh, give me a home where the buf-fal-o roam, where the deer and the an-tel-ope play, where sel-dom is heard a dis-cour-ag-ing

© Arranged 2019 for The Great Courses by Dave & Peg Dunbar.

"Home on the Range" [page 2]

© Arranged 2019 for The Great Courses by Dave & Peg Dunbar.

# LESSON 11

# *Onset: Engaging Balanced Tone*

**FEATURED SONG**

"Amazing Grace"

**EQUIPMENT NEEDED FOR VIDEO EXERCISES**

none

**LIST OF VIDEO EXERCISES**

- ❑ **EXERCISE 1**: Quarter-Note Pulse
- ❑ **EXERCISE 2**: Rolling Rs
- ❑ **EXERCISE 3**: Clean Onset
- ❑ **EXERCISE 4**: Siren and Staccato
- ❑ **EXERCISE 5**: Assisting Consonants
- ❑ **EXERCISE 6**: Vocal Fry and Yawn-Sigh

You are now ready to explore making intentional sound—starting at the beginning, with the way you engage with tone at the top of a phrase. This is called the onset. The ideal initiation of sound creates a clear, clean tone that's free of pressure and breathiness. Finding the perfect balance of energy is important to getting a clear tone with the voice.

# Ways to Start Tone

A great onset is the ultimate expression of dynamic equilibrium. At the onset, you are tapping into an energy that is already moving. This energy is a delicate, energized, and specific energy—like releasing a spinning top. You must let it release specifically without pressure.

The idea of appoggio can really help you find your easy, dynamic equilibrium. You don't want the abdominal area to pump in or push out as the tone starts, but you will feel the body responding and engaging with energy and specificity.

In order to achieve this clarity, it is important to use the imagination and intention to prepare the vocal mechanism for function and ease. A complete release before the easy onset is critical to success. It is important to be as invested in the energy of the silence between notes as you are with the onset of tone.

To get a clear and even tone, you need to be sure that energy is evenly distributed, both in the release before and in the engagement—the moment of onset.

In looking for your most balanced onset, you can explore the full spectrum of ways to start tone. On one end of the spectrum, you can start your sound with lots of air being passed through open vocal folds. This is called aspiration. Starting tone this way sounds like [h]. The vocal folds separate before they come together, allowing air to flow through the folds, often creating a breathy tone. The aspirate consonant, *h*, is an example of a time when we expect the folds to separate. But be careful that you are only using aspiration when your text calls for it rather than on every note.

Explore sounds on this end of the spectrum. Speak "ha." Now sing it, allowing the tone to be influenced by the aspirate consonant, *h*. Here you've chosen to intentionally keep the cords separated, allowing the tone to continue to be breathy. Generally, this is something you want to avoid in singing. A breathy tone can lead to fatigue over time and is limited in color options. If you find that your tone is generally breathy, working on onset exercises are critical for your success.

On the other end of the spectrum, you can engage with a hard glottal—something that misplaces the ease and flexibility of the tone. Glottal sounds are used a lot in the English language, but they don't need to be pressurized or hard. Try to find your hardest glottal. Pretend that you are annoyed and say "uh." Now try singing "uh." This pressurized version of tone initiation is costly over time. While you may use it sparingly in your work, starting each phrase with a hard glottal can be very fatiguing. Again, if you find that this end of the spectrum is closest to your current onset approach, work with onset exercises for a more balanced neutral.

Think of a kid who has just intentionally dropped food on the floor and innocently says "uh-oh." Say it like that—in a strong, glottal way. Now imagine you are delightfully surprised and say "uh-oh"—in an aspirated, breathy way (more like "huh-ho"). Can you see how the feeling is easy, almost like an inhalation, rather than a heavy, pressurized tone? This is clean and clear and uses minimal effort. Can you hear the neat, clean, and clear tone that's produced?

Now just imagine that you are going to say "uh-oh," but don't actually let any sound escape. Can you feel the vocal folds coming together? This is the preparation that's necessary for easy, clean phonation. The release before is equally important, so you don't want to anticipate too much!

As you work toward a clean, dynamic onset, it will be critical that you listen for what your voice needs in order to find balance. Where do you fall on the spectrum? If you are pressing, you can utilize the [h] sound to help you release glottal pressure, temporarily swinging the pendulum to introduce a new way of connecting to the start of tone. If you are finding that your tone tends to be breathy, you can engage with a gentle glottal to swing your pendulum toward more clarity.

Style, language, word stress, character, and pitch all can affect what kind of onset you choose to use. The idea of this lesson is to create an understanding of the most efficiently balanced onset available for you. The goal is for you to find a healthy baseline that you can use to ground your choices. You will be able to swing your pendulum whatever way you choose for artistic reasons and will be capable of finding your neutral with ease and confidence.

Each of us has individual habits and vocal qualities. If you are finding that you tend to be breathy or overaspirate or if you tend to overpressurize or use heavy glottals, choose the video exercises that support your current needs and goals.

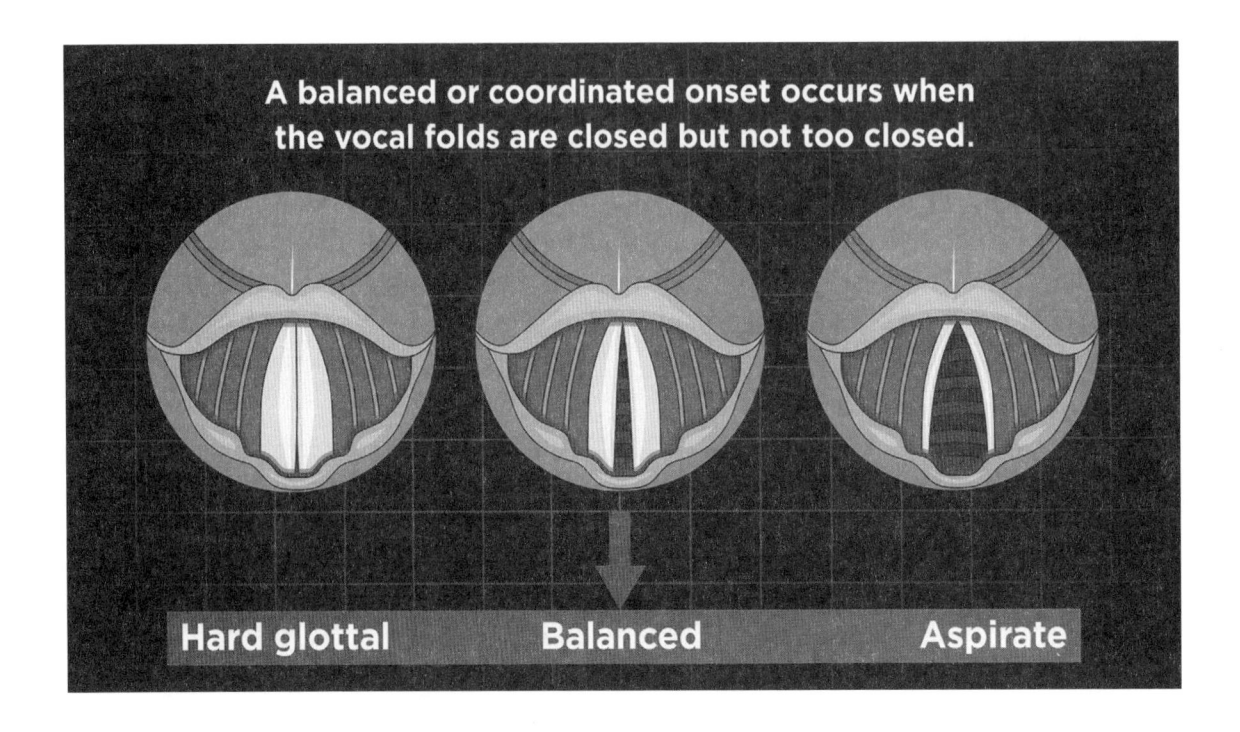

**A balanced or coordinated onset occurs when the vocal folds are closed but not too closed.**

Hard glottal — Balanced — Aspirate

# Practicing Onset

The song for this lesson, "Amazing Grace,"* was written in 1773 and remains one of the most recognizable songs in the United States today. Here's the first line:

>Amazing Grace, how sweet the sound

Notice that the first word of the song starts with a vowel. You'll want to think about your "uh-oh" feel. The *g* on the word *grace* has a harder glottal feel than any other English consonant, and the word *how* engages with the aspirate consonant, *h*.

Start completely without consonants first, finding your most beautiful onset for each phrase. In fact, use your "uh" of "uh-oh" for every note to start. Do this for the first verse. You don't have to rearticulate the onset for every note—keep it legato, or smooth and connected. Simply reset after each inhalation.

Now try the actual vowels of the song for the first verse. Speak one phrase—the first line of the song—focusing on just vowels. Then, take a full inhalation and sing on those vowels.

Continue the whole first verse, phrase by phrase, in this manner.

How did that go? Notice that if you start the phrase with an easy onset, the rest of the phrase is quite easy. If you find as you ascend that you feel more pressure, feel free to stop and reset the onset to find your easiest expression of phonation for the note and vowel.

Remember your dynamic posture; deep, released inhalation; and easy, clean onset. Now sing the first verse of "Amazing Grace" with text, looking for the clear, easy onset that leads to free vibration throughout.

>Amazing Grace, how sweet the sound
>That saved a wretch like me.
>I once was lost but now am found
>Was blind but now I see.

Feel free to work through the second verse on your own (and other verses if you like!). Practice any moments that challenge you. While you practice, ask yourself a few questions: Are you finding better balance in your tone? Are you aware of how your onset sets you up for singing the full phrase?

---

\* "Amazing Grace" was written as a Christian hymn and carries a message of forgiveness and acceptance. But the message of the song has become universal even within the secular realm. It weaves gratitude and hope with despair.

# Amazing Grace

Music based on "New Britain," an English folk song
Lyrics by John Newton

Arranged by
Dave & Peg Dunbar

**Larghetto**

A -
Through

maz - ing grace, how sweet the sound that saved a
man - y dan - gers, toils, and snares, I have al -

wretch like me! I once was lost but
read - y come; 'twas faith that brought me

© Arranged 2019 for The Great Courses by Dave & Peg Dunbar.

"Amazing Grace"  [page 2]

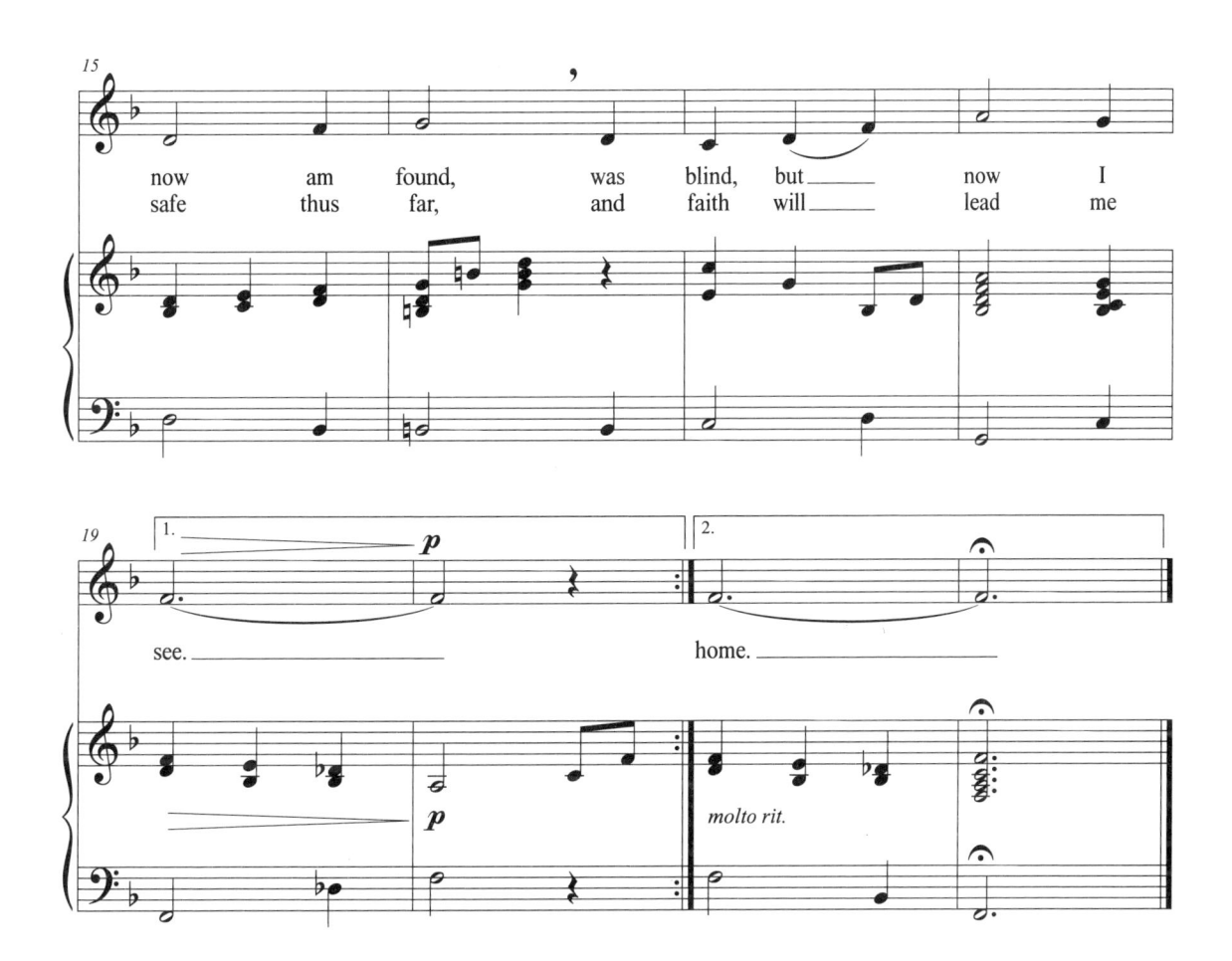

# LESSON 12

# Resonance: Exploring Vocal Colors

**FEATURED SONG**

"I Softly Sing"

**EQUIPMENT NEEDED FOR VIDEO EXERCISES**

none

**LIST OF VIDEO EXERCISES**

- **EXERCISE 1**: Smirk
- **EXERCISE 2**: Nose Plug
- **EXERCISE 3**: On Your Head
- **EXERCISE 4**: Hung-A
- **EXERCISE 5**: Nose Plug and Sing
- **EXERCISE 6**: Singing on Your Head

Have you noticed how sound travels differently in different spaces, such as a large room with tile walls versus a smaller carpeted room? Sound waves travel and bounce off surfaces like a ball bounces on the ground. Generally, sound bounces best off smooth, hard surfaces. Imagine the difference between bouncing a basketball on a polished gym floor versus your bed. This bouncing is called resonance.

# Internal Resonance Pathways

Nearly every musical instrument has a resonator. Any container of air that amplifies part of the vibrations moving through the air is a resonator. The air inside a violin, guitar, or piano acts as a resonator for the vibrating strings.

Sound vibration travels inside your mechanism, too! The amazing and unique thing about the vocal mechanism is that every instrument is completely unique and can actively change shape.

After your tone is created by breath engaging with your vocal cords, this vibration excites air molecules, setting up resonant frequencies in your internal space before it exits your body for all to hear. In other words, the vocal tract acts as a resonator and filter for sound created by the vocal folds. This pathway between the larynx and lips is an important determinant in the quality of emitted sound. Just like your fingerprint, your internal makeup has lots of individual properties that distinguish the sound or timbre of your unique voice.

The average length of a vocal tract is about 17 centimeters for males and 14 centimeters for females. In addition to gender, DNA, hormones, deviations, allergies, environment, and age affect your voice. So not only will your voice be unique to you, but you will also go through several variations of your voice in your lifetime.

Perhaps most interesting and exciting for singers, you can train, shape, and control many of the internal resonance pathways. It is one of the areas that singers can influence to create the sounds they are looking for.

Of course, it is also the space that allows us to create and distinguish language!

Think of this pathway between the vocal folds and your mouth as a filter for the sound heard by others. As a trained singer, you can exert control over this filter to create the sounds you would like to produce. Much of the technical work you do as a singer focuses on balancing this configuration. You work on your vowels and consonants, but there are variations even within vowel-formation space.

As a singer, you are looking beyond language. You are also aiming for beautiful sound—for the so-called singer formant, which is a frequency peak in the resonance spectrum. Essentially, it is the ring that is experienced when everything is balanced for a particular voice on a particular note and particular vowel. It generally carries well, echoing much like a voice in a stairwell.

Small physical adjustments to the vocal tract can make extreme changes. Moving the tongue or lips just a millimeter can create entirely different sounds. This process requires a lot of fine muscle coordination and is where singers dedicate most of their time and energy. The muscles around the vocal tract can flex and relax, changing the shape of the space, creating different colors and sounds.

---

Resonate *literally means "to re-sound."*

# Controlling and Shaping Resonance

Up until this lesson, we've primarily explored the respiratory and phonatory systems. This lesson moves into discussing the resonatory system. There are three main areas of resonance: the nasal cavities, the oral cavity, and the pharyngeal cavity. From the outside, you may think that the bones of your skull are massive and solid. In reality, many of them are hollow shells.

- The spaces from the roof of your mouth toward the top of your head are comprised of your nasal cavities. They are also called sinuses, and they allow space for internal vibration.

- The oral cavity—your mouth—is comprised of the space between the roof of your mouth and your jaw. It is highly variable in shape and dimension from person to person and moment to moment, depending on the status of the lips, tongue, jaw, cheeks, and velum (or soft palate). Movement of these areas results in modification of the size and acoustic characteristics of the oral cavity.

- The pharyngeal cavity is the space from the base of your skull to around the sixth cervical vertebrae. It sits behind the nasal and oral cavities and goes down to the epiglottis. The pharynx is often divided into three cavities: the nasopharynx, the oropharynx, and the laryngopharynx.* Many of the muscles you can sense in the pharyngeal space are constrictor muscles—so the more relaxed these muscles are, the more space you create.

How do we gain access to controlling and shaping our resonance?

This is where articulation and resonance systems intersect. Our direct control of our articulators—lips, tongue, teeth, and soft palate—is a major tool for adjusting the acoustic properties of the vocal tract.

Where in your body should you place the sound?

We can create the container for the sound to vibrate, but typically the more you try to place and manipulate the actual vibration, the less vibrant your tone will become. You can feel the sensations of sound and use those sensations to monitor the sounds you produce, but placement isn't reliable or desirable for creating sound. So focus on creating the container for vibration and explore the options.

Everyone has their personal preference for sound; you can record and listen to yourself to find your preferences. The important thing is to explore what colors and sounds you have available to you. In this lesson, you are going to function from a more-is-better place when it comes to internal space. This is only to encourage exploration and stretch and may or may not land in what your personal sound preference is. Ultimately, you are looking for a balance.

In the Italianate school of singing, the color balance of sound is described as

---

* The nasopharynx sits above the soft palate, behind the nasal cavities. The oropharynx is between the soft palate and the hyoid bone, sitting behind the oral cavity. The laryngopharynx is between the hyoid bone and the esophagus, so it refers even to the space at levels below the level of the vocal folds! Movement of the tongue and larynx affects this space.

chiaroscuro, meaning the light and the dark, the ping and the boom, the front and the back, etc. There are many ways to describe these sounds in the world of singing. Most importantly, you are aiming to maintain a well-balanced resonance throughout the range, regardless of vowel or pitch.

And remember that how you hear your voice in your head is not how others experience your voice, so don't be afraid to explore even the sounds that don't sound great in your head! In addition, it is important to understand that the source of sound is not the same as the sensation of sound. When you like something you hear on your recording of your lessons and practice, rewind and work to recreate the same sensation. Be careful not to shift your goal to recreating the same sound; the results may, and likely will, differ.

## Checking Your Nasality

Think of the soft palate as a traffic cop for resonance. The height of the soft palate modifies the shape of the vocal tract and therefore the sound of the mechanism. In particular, lifting the soft palate helps to block a nasal sound.

To check your nasality, you can plug your nose while singing vowels. You should be able to sing comfortably and beautifully without pressure leaning against the nose.

Sing through this lesson's song, "I Softly Sing," once to get a feel for it. Then, sing it just on vowels with your nose plugged. Don't try to sing it with consonants, many of which require a palate drop and rely on the nasal cavity resonance for their unique sounds.

What kind of space can you feel internally? Now sing all the way through the song normally and see how much more open and resonant you can feel when maintaining awareness of your internal spaces.

## HOMEWORK

Keep working on the exercises in the video lesson and get comfortable with maintaining an open, resonant internal space.

# I Softly Sing

Lyrics from "The Gift to Sing" by
James Weldon Johnson

Music by
Dave & Peg Dunbar

# LESSON 13

# *Utilizing the Soft Palate*

**FEATURED SONG**

"The Water Is Wide"

**EQUIPMENT NEEDED FOR VIDEO EXERCISES**

- straw
- glass of water
- mirror
- breath-freshening strips or mints
- yoga mat

**LIST OF VIDEO EXERCISES**

- **EXERCISE 1**: Nose Plug
- **EXERCISE 2**: Finding More Internal Space
- **EXERCISE 3**: Lifting the Palate with Consonant Shifts
- **EXERCISE 4**: Palate Chaser
- **EXERCISE 5**: Mirror Look
- **EXERCISE 6**: Singing with Palate Chaser
- **EXERCISE 7**: On Your Head

Isn't it funny that even the mention of a yawn can make you yawn? A yawn is an involuntary coordinated movement of the diaphragm, thoracic cavity, larynx, and soft palate. When it comes to singing, a yawn is sometimes used to teach a lifted palate, as yawning is a good involuntary way to wake it up. However, a yawn also leads to a lot of tension in the tongue and is more of a stretch than a lifted position, but it can be useful to help you understand the location of the palate.

# Activating the Soft Palate

Try running the tip of your tongue along the top of your mouth, starting with the tip of your tongue behind the front teeth, and tracing it back toward the soft palate.* The upper ridge is the hard palate. Eventually, you'll feel the tissue turn soft—this is your soft palate. If you open your mouth and look in the mirror, you will likely see your uvula† hanging down from the center of the soft palate.

Our soft palate is responsible for closing the nasal passages during swallowing, keeping food out of the respiratory tract. During sneezing, it can protect your nasal passages by diverting some of the gunk into the mouth.

Now yawn to try to activate the soft palate. Focus on the beginning of the yawn. This feeling certainly activates a lift and is related to what it feels like to have a good laryngeal and palate position. Unfortunately, as the yawn progresses, it adds tension.

While yawning can help you feel what it means to activate the palate, something that's a bit more productive for singing is using the idea of surprise or excitement. Both are great to evoke a palate lift that's free of tension. Simply imagine something that would shock you with delight and make a shocked face.

In singing, you can think of the soft palate as a traffic cop for resonance and articulation by telling them to go one way or the other. Remember, the soft palate is basically a portal to the nasal cavity.

There are several muscle groups that raise and lower the soft palate. During swallowing, it naturally rises to keep food and liquids out of the nasal cavity. As you talk, it moves up and down freely to create different vowels and consonants. Nasal sounds (such as [m] and [n]) require that it lowers so that sound gets filtered by the nose.

If it is raised, vibration stays in the pharynx and oral cavity. If it lowers, sound is dampened by the nasal cavity resonators. The nasal cavity creates specific sound characteristics that some like and some don't.

It is difficult to feel and engage in a lifted palate without tension, especially if you aren't used to thinking about it. Although it is useful to understand how the soft palate mechanism functions and to be sure your palate is functioning with agility, it is not necessarily something that every singer has to think about while singing. We all have very different anatomies.

If you have a combination of a large uvula and heavy tonsils, this could prevent you from getting a clear tone without a lifted palate. If this describes you, then learning to lift your palate is critical. You have to learn how to lift your palate and build strength and flexibility before the motion becomes natural in singing. On the other

---

\*     Be warned that this can initiate a gag reflex in many people.

†     The word *uvula* comes from Latin, meaning "small grape."

hand, some people can naturally lift the palate without thought.

Just like every other muscle in the body, the muscles that activate the soft palate can be trained no matter what their current condition. You can practice and retrain patterns, and eventually it won't require conscious attention. However, this takes time. Just know that having a flexible palate will reward you when it comes to singing.

If the soft palate is low, this will create a nasal sound. If the soft palate is stiff, it will create a monotonous tone without much flexibility.

Generally, the way the palate responds to changes in vowel and pitch is with tiny involuntary movements. To see how this works, look in the mirror, open your mouth, and imagine singing a high note. Does the palate lift? It should. But sometimes people build in habits over their lifetime that move them away from the most flexible natural movement.

## Lifting the Soft Palate

There are some exercises that you can do to work on building agility and flexibility in the palate so that it can learn to respond naturally while you are singing if it isn't already doing so.

You can always tell if the soft palate is raised by plugging your nose, as you explored in the previous lesson. If the sound changes or you feel a strong presence with your nose plugged verses not plugged, it is likely that the soft palate is lowered and sound is escaping through the nose cavity.

Grab a straw and a glass of water. When you drink through a straw, your palate will lift to prevent liquid from entering the nose. See if you can sense this as you drink. Can you hold the fluid in the straw? This also can help you find the internal sensation of a lifted palate.

Grab your smartphone or a flashlight and get in front of a mirror. Shine the light to the back of your throat and yawn. Did you see your palate move? Note how much flexibility there is in this area. Try taking a surprised breath. Can you keep the palate up? Next, sing a major scale with this same elevated and released palate.

Try singing the tune of this lesson's song, "The Water Is Wide," while watching your palate in the mirror. Be sure to maintain your alignment and utilize your breath with intention and energy. When do you notice that you want to drop your palate? Is there any correlation to how it feels to sing it? Do you feel more tension or effort when the palate drops? Just notice and play, reserving judgement.

### HOMEWORK

Continue to work on the exercises in the video lesson for the greatest long-term success and agility.

# The Water Is Wide

Traditional folk song  
Arranged by Dave & Peg Dunbar

*Andante*

1. The water is wide, _____ I can-not get o'er _____ and neith-er have _____ I wings to fly. _____ Build me a boat _____ that can car-ry

back _____ up a-gainst an oak, _____ think-ing it was _____ a trust-y tree, _____ but first it swayed _____ and _____ then it

hand - some and love is kind, _____ bright as a jew'l _____ when it is new; _____ but love grows old _____ and _____ wax - es

© Arranged 2019 for The Great Courses by Dave & Peg Dunbar.

"The Water Is Wide"   [page 2]

# LESSON 14

# *Releasing Jaw Tension*

### FEATURED SONG

"Scarborough Fair"

### EQUIPMENT NEEDED FOR VIDEO EXERCISES

- ❏ surgical gloves
- ❏ mirror
- ❏ cork or highlighter (optional)

### LIST OF VIDEO EXERCISES

- ❏ **EXERCISE 1**: Relaxing the Jaw
- ❏ **EXERCISE 2**: Internal Jaw Massage
- ❏ **EXERCISE 3**: Finding Your Neutral Jaw
- ❏ **EXERCISE 4**: Neutral Jaw with Tone
- ❏ **EXERCISE 5**: Neutral Jaw with Vowels
- ❏ **EXERCISE 6**: Neutral Jaw with Consonants
- ❏ **EXERCISE 7**: Reengaging the Jaw

The temporomandibular joint (TMJ) is the place where your jaw hinges from your skull. It is a joint that is used constantly—for speaking, eating, and singing. Add grinding your teeth at night and holding it when you are stressed to that list and you might end up overusing it. TMJ tension is one of the most common tensions singers experience.

# Jaw Tension

Why is jaw tension undesirable for singing, and why is it so common?

Any extrinsic muscle tension—but especially in this area, which is so close to where you are phonating—can lead to a tight sound. If the jaw is engaged while singing, the muscles around the larynx might get tight, limiting freedom in the vocal folds. Jaw tension can also inhibit the soft palate lift.

Sometimes what we identify as jaw tension is really more of a coordination issue. There is often interdependence with the tongue and lips. Most of us swallow and speak more than we sing, so those muscles are in the habit of working together. When we sing, we like to separate the functions of the jaw or teeth, tongue, and lips.

The jaw has two main parts: the upper jaw, or maxilla, which is a fused part of your skull, so it only moves when your whole head moves; and the lower jaw, or mandible, which is connected to the skull at the TMJ. This joint is highly versatile and can move up and down and side to side.

The two main muscles that control jaw movement are the temporalis and the masseter. To find your masseter, put your hands on your cheeks and relax your jaw, allowing for space between your teeth. Then, bring your teeth together and bite down. Notice the bulge in the back of your cheeks. That's the masseter muscle.* It's a useful muscle for eating but is less helpful when it comes to singing.

Now put your hands around your temples and bite down. Can you feel the bulge there as well? This is the temporalis. Many people don't realize how much of what happens with the temporalis involves the jaw.

When you open your mouth naturally, the TMJ serves as a hinge—this movement is called rotation. When you get to a certain point, the hinge can also release down—this is called translation. Place your hands on the side of your face at the joint, and if you focus while opening and closing your mouth, you'll be able to feel when it moves from rotation to translation.

Generally, while singing, you don't need to go past the rotation width. In fact, for singing, you should really only move what is necessary to make sounds. There are lots of ways to create our language sounds, but to allow for freedom, ease in resonance, and balance, less is more.

When working on jaw release, it is important to first take a moment to center the body. All the work you have done to address your posture from head to toe will help you with this work. When the body is not in alignment, especially the head and neck posture, the jaw muscles are more likely to engage in compensation.

---

*   Your masseter is considered one of the strongest muscles in your body based on its weight. With all the muscles of the jaw working together, it can apply up to 200 pounds of pressure on the molars!

# Checking in with Your Jaw

Check in with your jaw by gently holding it with your thumbs and forefingers. Encourage it to move up and down. If you get resistance, try to calm down, slow down, and consciously relax. Find freedom in your movement.

Next, you'll move the major muscles of the jaw, locate any extra tension, and do your best to help release it through massage. Jaw exercises can be very painful and require fine muscle coordination and focus, so it is best to be calm in your mind and energized in your body to do this work.

Start by massaging your temples (or temporalis) with small circles and slowly and gently moving down past your ears by the TMJ. At your ear, draw your fingers down to your jaw slowly, allowing your mouth to open. Then, move your hands under your chin and neck. Take your time, breathing and consciously releasing as much tension and holding as you can on every breath.

Next, turn your head to the side. In this position, you can see and feel a prominent muscle pop out of your neck. This is the sternocleidomastoid, and it is another muscle that is often related to jaw tension. It is another area that will benefit from gentle massage.

Feel where this muscle is with your thumb and forefinger. Tilt your head toward the side you are holding to release it as much as possible. Gently hold it and then slowly turn your head toward the center. Start just behind your ear and follow this large muscle down. You'll find that it moves toward the front to your sternum and clavicle, so you can release and massage these areas. Next, move into the shoulder area.

Repeat this on the other side. Take your time and explore your most comfortable way to access this area. You can move your arm across your body or do the same side.

If you find you are holding a lot of tension in this area, you can take it to the next level by putting on a surgical glove and exploring the release of internal muscles.† This can be intense work, so stop if it is too much. Be gentle with yourself and get professional help from a specialized therapist or doctor if you need it.

First, with your glove (or clean hand), gently put your forefinger into your mouth between the back molars and your cheek, turn your fingernail toward the teeth, palm facing away. Gently hold the finger in this space while gently opening and closing your mouth a few times. Pause with your mouth closed and breathe. Try the other side.

How are you feeling? Does your jaw feel less engaged?

Breathe and allow everything to release. Work on this daily and gently.

---

† This exercise is very effective for singers who carry a lot of jaw tension.

# Finding a Neutral Jaw Position

For singing, it is important to keep the hinge in the natural, neutral position to prevent disorders. Finding a neutral jaw position can be tricky if you haven't thought about it. All of us have slightly different natural positions, so it is hard to find something that works for everyone. The key is that you want your most-released closed mouth to release into the least amount of tension as you open.

Close your eyes and take a few deep breaths. Notice that your tongue naturally sits on the top of your mouth in addition to the bottom. On your next inhalation, maintain your tongue connection with the roof of your mouth, especially the front part of your tongue, and drop your jaw. Only drop the jaw as far as this will allow. Close your mouth again and repeat this several times. Explore how much release you can find each time. Beware of the jaw wanting to jut forward or pull back.

Then, after you've exhaled, leave your jaw where it is and release your tongue. This is your ideal jaw position; avoid shifting forward or back from this place. Take one breath in and out in this position; then, close and repeat the full exercise. Your jaw should be flexible, never locked. This exercise can give you a tool for finding your neutral jaw position without subscribing to a specific position.

Jaw tension requires time and attention to truly find release. Because the jaw does move as the teeth articulate consonants, sometimes it is hard to differentiate function from tension. Try singing the "Scarborough Fair" melody on your favorite vowel. Perhaps place one finger on your chin gently to monitor whether the jaw is shifting forward, backward, or from side to side. You ideally want to find your neutral release throughout.

Next, sing the "Scarborough Fair" melody, alternating between [ɑ] and [i] on every other note. Can the jaw be disengaged from your vowels? Just let it hang in your neutral position.

One thing you can think about while you are singing music is finding a gentle inward cheek smile. This can help to free the masseter muscle. It also gives you a pleasant, easy smile. Challenge yourself to maintain this easy smile while engaging in vowels and consonants associated with your piece.

If you really connect to jutting your jaw forward—the bulldog look—think about biting an apple. The way you open and prepare to take the bite might help you release the hinge more naturally.

Now sing the song with the actual vowels of the words. Can the jaw be disengaged?

Finally, sing it with consonants, maintaining awareness and release.

## HOMEWORK

At this point in the course, review the recordings you've been making of your singing to see just how far you've come.

# Scarborough Fair

Traditional English folk song  Arranged by Dave & Peg Dunbar

Are you go-ing to Scar-bo-rough Fair?
Have her make me a cam-bric shirt.
Have you been to Scar-bo-rough Fair?
When he's done and fin-ished his work,

Pars-ley, sage, rose-mar-y and thyme. Re-
Pars-ley, sage, rose-mar-y and thyme. With-
Pars-ley, sage, rose-mar-y and thyme. Re-
pars-ley, sage, rose-mar-y and thyme, ask

© Arranged 2019 for The Great Courses by Dave & Peg Dunbar.

"Scarborough Fair"   [page 2]

mem - ber me to one who lived there.
out no seams, nor fine need - le work.
mem - ber me from one who lives there.
him to come for his cam - bric shirt.

1., 2., 3.

She once was a true love of mine.
Then she'll be a true love of mine.
He once was a true love of mine.
Then he'll be a

4. *molto rit.*

true love of mine.

# LESSON 15

# Your Voice Type

**FEATURED SONG**

"Last Rose of Summer"

**EQUIPMENT NEEDED FOR VIDEO EXERCISES**

none

**LIST OF VIDEO EXERCISES**

- **EXERCISE 1**: Finding Your Passaggio
- **EXERCISE 2**: Finding Your Best Key

This lesson will introduce you to a general way to classify your vocal mechanism. You can use the following principles for repertoire-selection assistance at any age, but reevaluate often and don't stick yourself in any category permanently. While this can serve as a guide—and, most importantly, help you choose keys and songs that allow you to shine and feel comfortable—it is not meant to limit you or make you feel stuck.

*The classification of voice changes throughout life. The classifications presented in this lesson are general and might only apply to one period of your artistic work. Voices can take years to mature. In general, the lower and bigger the voice, the longer it tends to take to settle and mature.*

## Voice Classification and Range

Which voice type are you? Your anatomy will provide you with the basic foundation—the instrument you play. In the same way that a tuba cannot sound like a flute, you will do your best work if you play the instrument that you have. In other words, if you embrace your own instrument, you will have the most success.

There are as many arguments against classification as there are for it in the world of singing pedagogy. Whether it is important for a student to understand his or her classification is a huge debate. In general, many believe that classification is of interest more to the teacher than to the singer.

But in this day and age—especially if you are taking this course—you are both the singer and the teacher. Gone are the days of giving someone complete control of your voice by having daily or more frequent lessons. A teacher can impart information and give feedback, but you are the one responsible for applying and integrating it.

Understanding your voice and classification can help inform your work, but it perhaps should not be something you think about while you are singing. In many ways, it can help you embrace and love the mechanism you have, but you don't have to feel like a prisoner to your classification. Essentially, you want to sing in a range and choose repertoire that allows you to shine with your unique, individual voice.

So you don't want to feel stuck by your voice type, but sometimes the knowledge and understanding of your voice classification can free you. For example, when you're first starting voice work, your goal might be to expand your range or sing specific high notes, such as high Cs. When you understand that singing full-voice high Cs is normally something that only well-developed tenors and sopranos (a voice classification) can do, it helps this to be released from your uninformed goal list. If you are, in fact, a baritone (another classification), then the goal to sing full-voice high Cs will likely be a fruitless one, leading to tension and frustration. Perhaps a better goal would be to make the most of one's own mechanism, utilizing the full range available with healthy tone. It is a more attainable and healthy goal to work toward.

Range is the highest and lowest notes you can phonate, and the general range of each voice part can be different. For example, a mezzo-soprano might not have the physical ability to produce the tones that some high sopranos can produce beautifully and healthfully, but the mezzo-soprano might sing as high as some classifications of sopranos and sometimes lower than certain tenors.

Perhaps more important to understanding your voice type is tessitura, which is a little more complicated than range. Think of tessitura sort of like the mathematical mean of the notes. While tessitura isn't one number like the mean, to determine tessitura you look at where the bulk of the notes lie and sit across the piece, not as much at the extremes. It is the range in which most of the notes lie in a piece.

*Historically, in the classification system for singers, there is a gender binary and inherent gendered language that doesn't adequately or appropriately include those who identify differently.*

# Registration

The idea of registration, like so many things in singing, is widely controversial. What is meant by registration? As 19th-century pedagogue Manuel García says:

> By the word register, we mean a series of consecutive and homogeneous tones going from low to high, produced by the development of the same mechanical principle, and whose nature differs essentially from another series of tones, equally consecutive and homogeneous, produced by another mechanical principle.

Every voice has a wide range of options when it comes to registration. For example, a person might be able to sing extremely high in falsetto, but this doesn't mean that the singer is a soprano. Understanding where there is a register shift can serve as an indicator of voice type.

How many registrations are there?

Bass clef voices are commonly categorized as tenor, baritone, or bass. For bass clef singers, there are at least two clear registrations that are universally recognized: the chest voice and the falsetto. For treble voices, regularly categorized as soprano, mezzo-soprano, and contralto, there is a similar transition, but it is often less obvious and tends to be referred to as chest and head voice.

In the Western tradition of singing, we often try to even out the registration shifts for the listener. However, in some styles, it is very attractive to hear the registration shift. Either way, science shows that there is an actual shift in registration. In other words, these tones are fundamentally produced in a different way.

Note that while chest voice doesn't actually only occur in the chest, it is a widely used terminology to describe the tones created when the vocal cords are thickened by the thyroarytenoid muscles, resulting in a somewhat-square shape in the glottis and a significant vertical phase during the vibration cycle. This cycle can be expanded and utilized by choice—and it often is for specific styles, such as belting in musical theater.

The head voice (which doesn't only vibrate in the head), or falsetto, has a very different quality. Science shows that these tones rely more on the cricothyroid muscle and that the glottis is in more of a triangular shape. Perhaps most notable is that the vertical-phase differences are greatly reduced or perhaps not present in the head voice, or falsetto.

Again, this range can be expanded or developed, as is the case with a falsettist or countertenor, a category that has emerged and become more popular recently*. This is a singer who chooses to develop his or her falsetto voice, expanding his or her range and capabilities in that range and voice type.

Where the registration shifts naturally happen has a lot to do with voice classification. This is called the *zona di passaggio*, or "passage zone" in the classical singing tradition. While the word *passaggio* originated in the Italian school, it has become a universally utilized term in the study of singing. What pedagogue you follow will determine how many passaggios you might recognize in the voice, but for our introductory purposes, we can focus on the main one as an area of the voice, rather than labeling every moment of the shift.

Take your hand and put it on your chest. Speak normally. Can you feel a vibration in your chest? Now speak very high. You will notice the absence or lessening of this vibration. You are feeling the difference in registration.

Now put your hand on your chest and do an ascending siren, using your breath to feel the shifting zone of your mechanism. As you ascend, there will come a point where you might involuntarily start to raise the chin or lift the larynx and the chest vibration stops or lessens. Also, as you continue to ascend, often the quality of tone has an audible shift and the voice will either stop or switch into a falsetto or lightened head-voice tone. The space between where the start of the change happens through the release into the next register is the passaggio. In most voices, this manifests in about a range of a fourth. The location of where this shift happens is a big determiner in your voice classification.

---

*   During the 16th century, there was another voice type called the castrato that was introduced when women were banned from the stage and church choirs. It was most prominent in 17th-and 18th-century Italian opera. A castrato voice was created by castrating a male singer before puberty. The castration did not allow the voice to go through the registration shift and removed hormones that affected how the body grew. Castrati were reported to have enormous rib cages and unique physical stature, producing voices of extraordinary power and agility in the treble range. This practice was made illegal in 1870, so this classification no longer exists.

## LESSON 15—YOUR VOICE TYPE

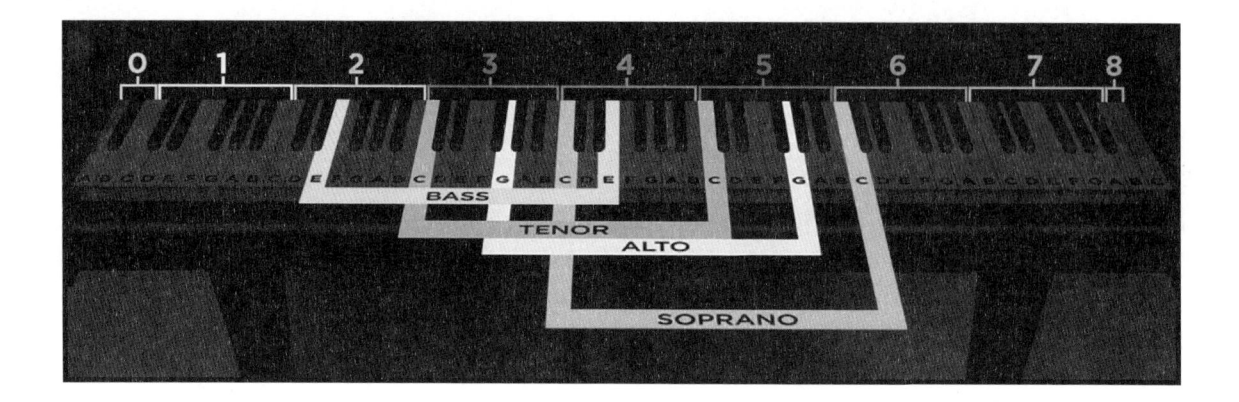

Depending on how deep you want to get into voice classification, you can break it down anywhere from four common voice types—soprano, alto, tenor, and bass—to hundreds of classifications. And because our voices are as unique as our fingerprints, the classifications develop from describing our nature rather than us all truly fitting into a specific classification.

So, why classify at all?

It is helpful to know your basic classification and understand your passaggio when you are choosing repertoire and developing and managing your register shifts. It essentially helps you make sense of the developing mechanisms and informs your decisions about what to sing. Finding the keys that feel the most comfortable for you can make all the difference.

For our purposes, we are simply going to focus on high-, middle-, and low-voice categories because it is common for publishers to produce songbooks in high and low keys, or medium-high and medium-low keys, or high, medium, and low keys. In addition, if you are purchasing books designed for soprano, mezzo-soprano, contralto, tenor, baritone, or bass, you can likely deduce that soprano and tenor are high, mezzo and baritone are medium, and alto or contralto and bass are low.

Despite some cultural pressures, know that higher isn't necessarily better! We all have high and low notes in our registers, and one person's high and low might be different than yours.

---

*As you approach a new piece, try as many keys as you can find. You don't want your category to define you; you want your technical facility and ability to lead the categorization. And know that a voice professional can help you with your categorization.*

# Identifying Your Voice Type

The video lesson can help you determine your natural passaggio as a singer. Notice when and if you feel a shift in registration while doing the exercise featured in the video. Note what pitch you are on when you feel the shift, especially if you feel that you *must* shift—this is the extreme edge, when the thyroarytenoid muscles reach their limit. Make sure to take note where in the range it occurs.

Remember that these are ranges and general guidelines and not rules for you and your unique voice. Registers can and will overlap, just like the speed for different gears in a car.

In order for you to explore your voice type and range, different keys are provided for this lesson's song, "Last Rose of Summer." Try them all and decide what feels and sounds the best for you. Is it in line with what your initial thoughts were with classification? None of the keys are better or worse, but they may be a better or worse fit for each individual. Get used to exploring different keys and repertoire to find what fits you and your unique gifts best!

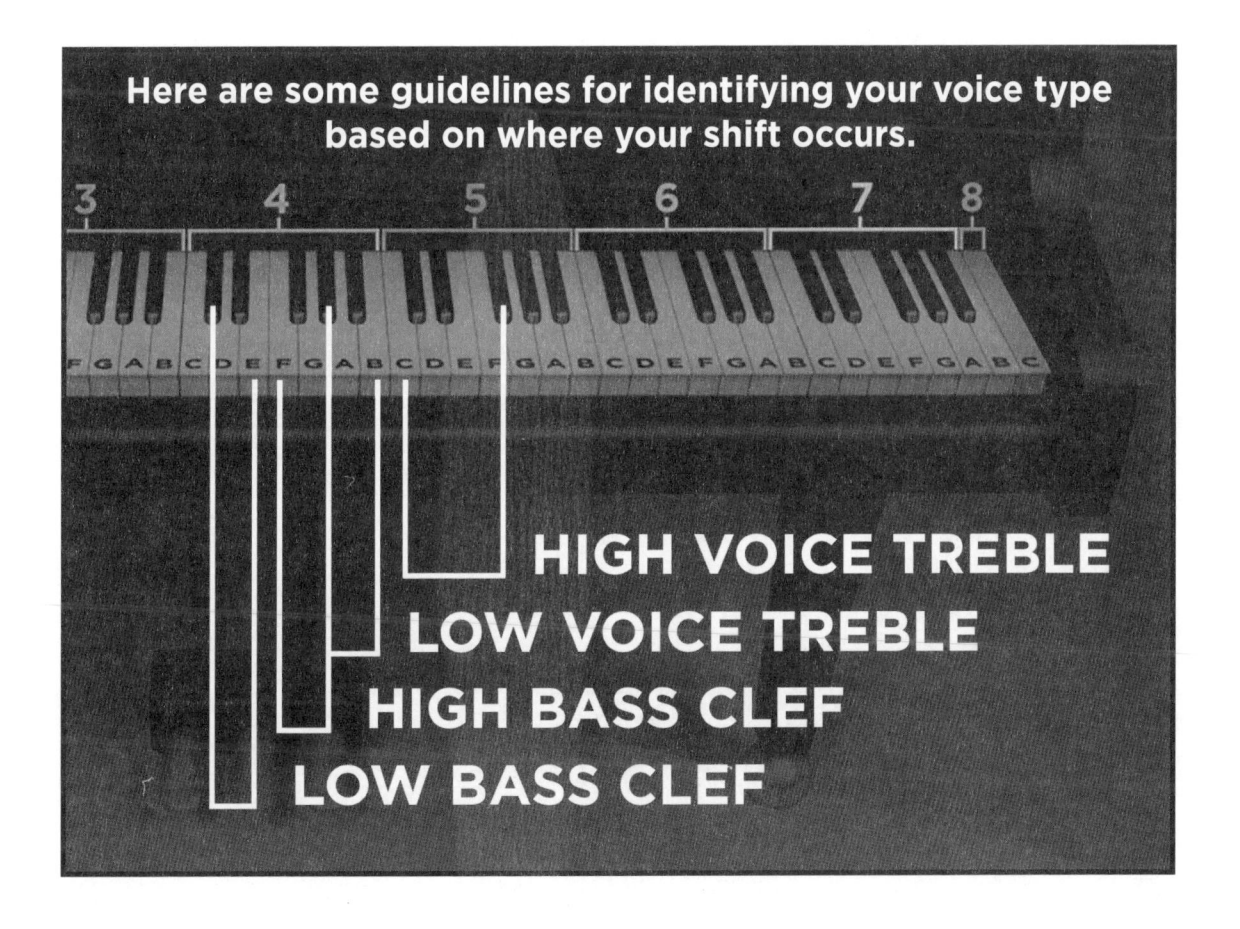

**Here are some guidelines for identifying your voice type based on where your shift occurs.**

- HIGH VOICE TREBLE
- LOW VOICE TREBLE
- HIGH BASS CLEF
- LOW BASS CLEF

# Last Rose of Summer

*(in A Major)*

Traditional Irish tune
Lyrics by Thomas Moore

Arranged by
Dave & Peg Dunbar

"Last Rose of Summer" in A Major   [page 2]

# Last Rose of Summer

*(in B-flat Major)*

Traditional Irish tune
Lyrics by Thomas Moore

Arranged by
Dave & Peg Dunbar

'Tis the last rose of summer, left blooming alone; all her lovely companions are faded and gone; no flower of her

© Arranged 2019 for The Great Courses by Dave & Peg Dunbar.

"Last Rose of Summer" in B-flat Major   [page 2]

# Last Rose of Summer

(in C Major)

Traditional Irish tune  
Lyrics by Thomas Moore

Arranged by  
Dave & Peg Dunbar

**Expressively** ♩ = 66

'Tis the last rose of sum- mer, left bloom- ing a - lone; all her love- ly com- pan- ions are fad - ed and gone; no flow - er of her

© Arranged 2019 for The Great Courses by Dave & Peg Dunbar.

"Last Rose of Summer" in C Major   [page 2]

© Arranged 2019 for The Great Courses by Dave & Peg Dunbar.

# Last Rose of Summer
*(in D Major)*

Traditional Irish tune
Lyrics by Thomas Moore

Arranged by
Dave & Peg Dunbar

"Last Rose of Summer" in D Major   [page 2]

kin - dred, no rose - bud is nigh, to re - flect back her blush - es, to give sigh for sigh.

© Arranged 2019 for The Great Courses by Dave & Peg Dunbar.

# Last Rose of Summer

*(in E Major)*

Traditional Irish tune  
Lyrics by Thomas Moore

Arranged by  
Dave & Peg Dunbar

'Tis the last rose of summer, left blooming alone; all her lovely companions are faded and gone; no flower of her

© Arranged 2019 for The Great Courses by Dave & Peg Dunbar.

"Last Rose of Summer" in E Major   [page 2]

# Last Rose of Summer

*(in F Major)*

Traditional Irish tune
Lyrics by Thomas Moore

Arranged by
Dave & Peg Dunbar

© Arranged 2019 for The Great Courses by Dave & Peg Dunbar.

"Last Rose of Summer" in F Major   [page 2]

© Arranged 2019 for The Great Courses by Dave & Peg Dunbar.

# Last Rose of Summer

(in F-sharp Major)

Traditional Irish tune
Lyrics by Thomas Moore

Arranged by
Dave & Peg Dunbar

'Tis the last rose of sum- mer, left bloom- ing a - lone; all her love- ly com- pan- ions are fad - ed and gone; no flow - er of her

"Last Rose of Summer" in F-sharp Major   [page 2]

# Last Rose of Summer
*(in G Major)*

Traditional Irish tune
Lyrics by Thomas Moore

Arranged by
Dave & Peg Dunbar

**Expressively** ♩ = 66

'Tis the last rose of sum- mer, left bloom- ing a- lone; all her love- ly com- pan- ions are fad- ed and gone; no flow- er of her

"Last Rose of Summer" in G Major   [page 2]

© Arranged 2019 for The Great Courses by Dave & Peg Dunbar.

# LESSON 16

# *Maximizing Your Vocal Range*

**FEATURED SONG**

"The Star-Spangled Banner"

**EQUIPMENT NEEDED FOR VIDEO EXERCISES**

none

**LIST OF VIDEO EXERCISES**

- ❑ **EXERCISE 1:** Safe and Effective Neck Massage
- ❑ **EXERCISE 2:** Extending Your Range with Scales

As you learned in the previous lesson, your natural vocal mechanism will have a certain natural tessitura, and many things can affect it over time (such as environment, hormones, etc.). However, in general, you can learn to expand your natural range with regular practice and solid technique. In other words, range is essentially determined but can be developed and maximized.

# Expanding Your Range

Generally, the pitch of a person's voice is determined by the resonant frequency of the vocal folds. In an adult bass clef voice, this frequency averages about 125 hertz, as the vocal cords of a bass clef voice are generally longer—around the size of a quarter in length. Adult treble voices produce around 210 hertz, with their cord size somewhere between a dime and a nickel. In children, the frequency is more than 300 hertz.

In addition to gender, there are variants from person to person. Because technical ability, agility, and practice can expand range, testing range can be tricky. Remember when you wrote down how high and low you could phonate in lesson 1? Now is a good time to try that exercise again and compare, seeing if you have already made a change with all of the singing and practicing you've done.

Do an arpeggio on your favorite closed trill (lip, tongue, or lip-tongue). Go as high and as low as you possibly can, note your highest and lowest note, and compare to how high and low you went in lesson 1. Have the notes changed? It is OK either way; it is just fun to note!

What is your basic range? Bass clef voices, note where you flip into falsetto—sometimes the falsetto has a whole new range of its own! Some treble voices also have something similar to a falsetto where they move into what is called a whistle tone.

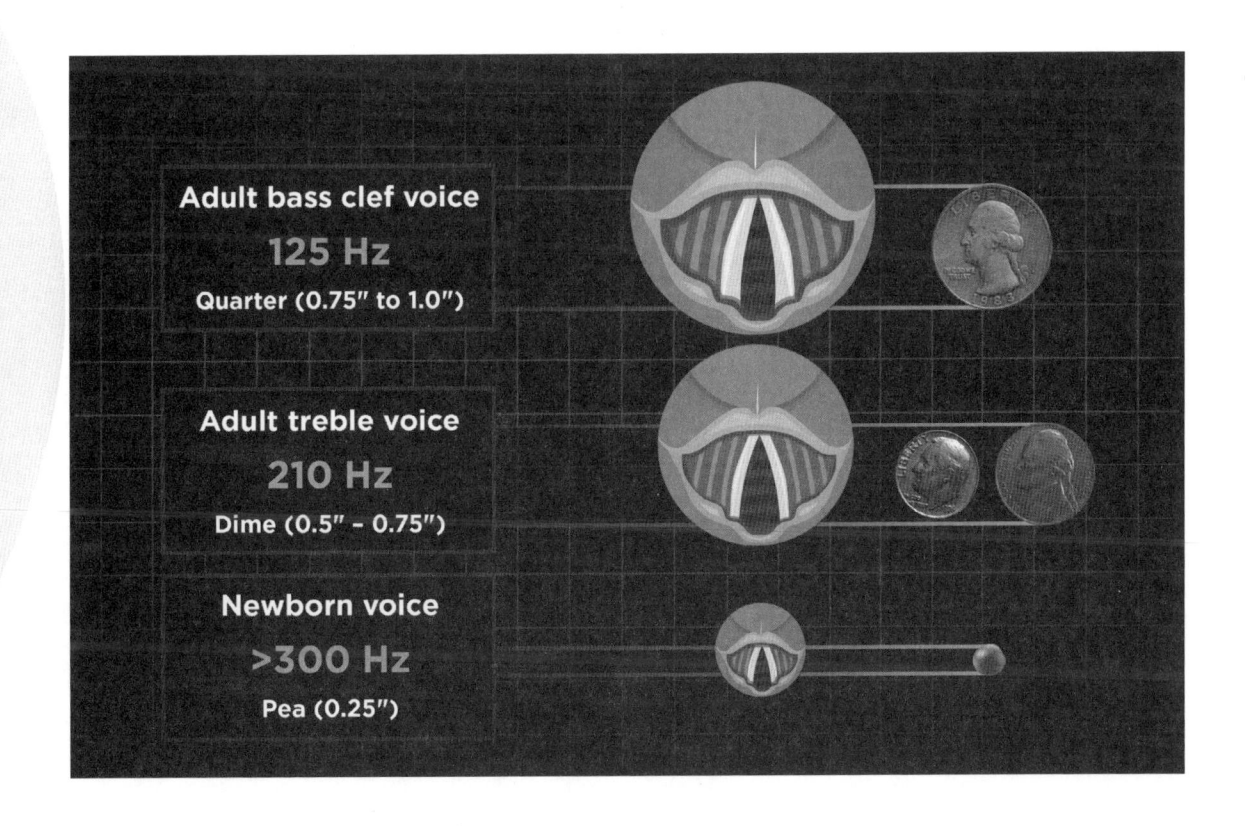

**Adult bass clef voice**
**125 Hz**
Quarter (0.75" to 1.0")

**Adult treble voice**
**210 Hz**
Dime (0.5" – 0.75")

**Newborn voice**
**>300 Hz**
Pea (0.25")

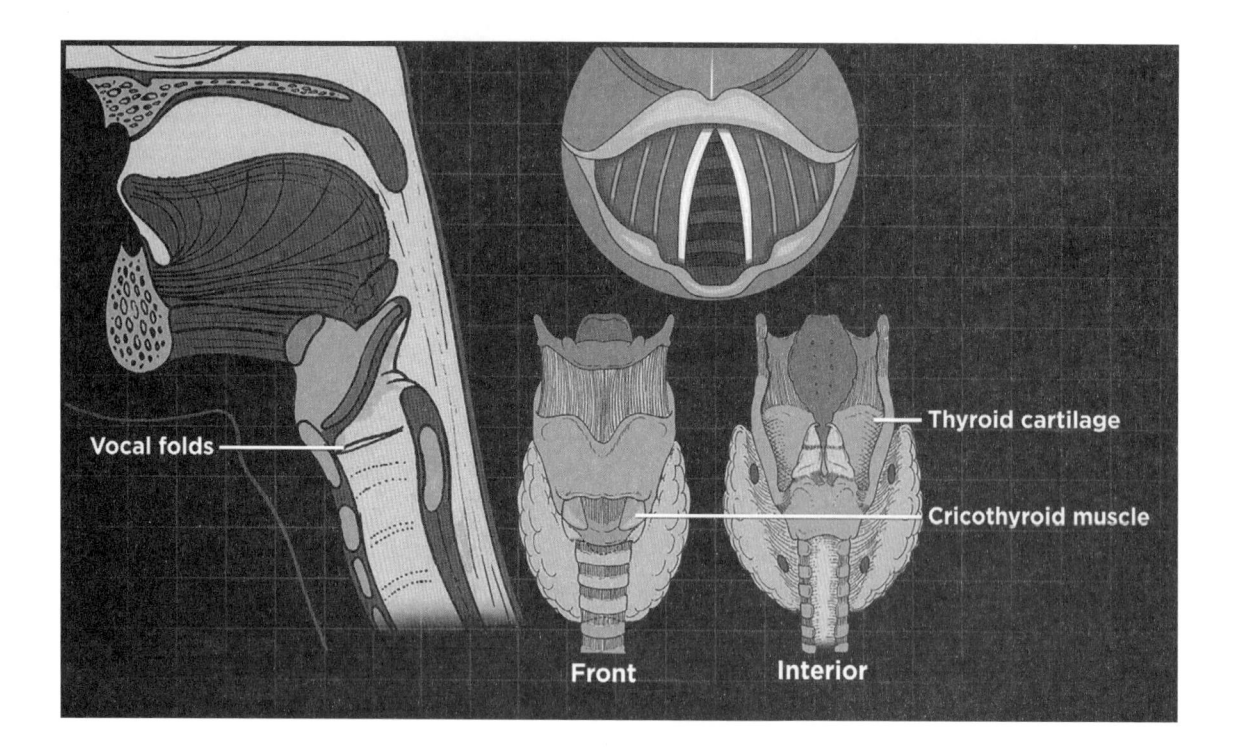

**Vocal folds** — **Thyroid cartilage** — **Cricothyroid muscle**

Front   Interior

Once the middle octave of the voice (from middle C up to high G) is well established, the extensions above and below tend to develop naturally. If you can stabilize and iron out the transitions in the voice for this middle octave, it tends to unlock some range automatically. As you work on the extensions, accessing the top tends to help the bottom, and opening the bottom tends to help the top.

One of the first things to address when working on expanding your range is your anxiety about range and pitch. Many students say they are afraid of high notes. Fear will certainly introduce tension, unground your breath, and produce blocks when attempting to make change.

Be willing to make some less-than-successful attempts when approaching range. Perhaps step away from your pitch pipe or piano to play with what your voice can do rather than letting note names dictate and decide. If you have perfect pitch, do a lot of sirens and sliding, allowing yourself to play and grow even with the knowledge of where you are and have been.

How high and low you can sing is determined in part by genetics and in part by the range of motion you are able to access at the cricothyroid joints. When the cricothyroid muscles tilt the thyroid cartilage forward, they lengthen your vocal folds.

# Self-Massage for Flexibility

You need maximum flexibility in all of the muscles and joints around the larynx to extend your range. To help with flexibility, you can engage in self-massage of those muscles.

Find your thyroid cartilage—that little protrusion that we call the Adam's apple at the front of the neck. Gently place your fingers on either side of your larynx, remembering that the hyoid bone sits right at the front of the larynx. Be really careful when you are working in this area.

First, give the larynx a slow, gentle wiggle. How does it feel? Does it move easily? Next, stabilize the larynx gently with your thumb and forefinger and then turn your head slowly and carefully to one side. Then, return to the center. Then, go the other direction, and return to center. Do this several times slowly.

Next, tilt the head toward the ceiling and gently massage down around the larynx, running a gentle stroke down.

Now go a little wider and farther back near the chin for a little more release around the hyoid bone, rocking gently back and forth, releasing and relaxing while you massage.

Finally, massage the back of the neck at the base of the skull. You don't want the digastric muscle to tense because it can tug on the larynx. Make small, relaxed circles on the back of your neck. You can actually do a siren or sing a passage while massaging these muscles, but don't try to make sound while working on the front. You can visit a licensed speech therapist if you are feeling a lot of resistance or think you need more or deeper work in this area.

The video exercises work on expanding and uniting your range. In all of the exercises, only go as high and as low as you feel comfortable. Stop when you need to. It is OK to feel a tiny stretch on the top and bottom of your range, but avoid any strain or discomfort. Most importantly, keep everything you've learned in mind: Maintain a dynamic spine and head posture, keep internal space flexible, and avoid jaw, tongue, and neck tension.

Note that it takes more concentrated breath energy to sing high than to sing low. When ascending, there is a gradual elongation of the vocal folds, creating an increase in vocal fold resistance to airflow. This reverses in descending pitches.

# Practicing in Your Range

For this lesson, the United States of America's national anthem—"The Star-Spangled Banner"—is the piece you'll explore. Because it has a large range and lots of leaps, the key might matter more than with some of the other pieces you've encountered in this course. In addition, it is a fairly advanced piece to sing, so with all of the wonderful work you've put in at this point, it will be an appropriate challenge!

Four versions of this song are included, so choose the key that feels the most comfortable. Know that you can sing this in any key—and people do. This will just be a good way to see what feels best to you.

This piece was originally composed in C but is probably most often performed in B-flat.

It is likely that the highest note in the piece, no matter which key you choose, will be challenging, partly because it is high and partly because it will feel high because of how it is approached—from the bottom and then arriving on a closed vowel! You will need to practice this piece for several weeks at least to really find comfort and mastery.

Remember, it takes more concentrated breath energy to sing high than to sing low. When ascending, there is a gradual elongation of the vocal folds, creating an increase in vocal fold resistance to airflow. This reverses in descending pitches.

Generally, lower notes need less stretched space, so be careful not to over-open or overblow as you go lower. A key to singing beautifully is to allow everything to be moving and flexible. If you give too much energy to the low notes, you will run out of steam as you go higher.

Now work through this piece phrase by phrase.

> O say can you see, by the dawn's early light,

Phrasing this together sets up a deep breath for the next phrase.

> What so proudly we hail'd at the twilight's last gleaming,

Keep this phrase long and connected. As you go to the end of this phrase, allow yourself to feel the tone more forward, resisting the temptation to over-space or overblow in the bottom of the range.

The next two phrases utilize the same melody contour as the first two, so apply the same ideas as you sing them.

> Whose broad stripes and bright stars through the perilous fight
> O'er the ramparts we watch'd were so gallantly streaming?

Now things are going to change. You are no longer starting in downward motion; you will ascend and go into a higher tessitura. Change the phrase length to represent the comma and to honor the higher tessitura. So perhaps breathe after *glare* but then connect "the bombs bursting in air, gave proof through the night that our flag was still there." Because this part of the song descends throughout, maybe you can do those last three pieces together. Give it a shot!

> And the rocket's red glare, the bombs bursting in air,
> Gave proof through the night that our flag was still there,

You should be at the end of your breath if you chose to do that, so don't panic if you are! Remember, you are setting yourself up for a deep breath for the next phrase. And if you can't do it the first time, it is OK! You can likely work up to it.

Think of the next phrase as the calm before the storm—resting up and preparing for the big one. So be careful not to overblow or stack the breath.

> O say does that star-spangled banner yet wave

After *wave*, take your time to truly release and relax in anticipation of the high note to come. In the United States, it has become tradition to sustain *free* and take a breath after it, but know that this detail and others are just guidelines as you find your own version. Remember on *free* to release the jaw and really let the [i] vowel be formed in your tongue. This can be a good one to try on your head if you are having trouble accessing the high note. This note likely sits above your passaggio, so it might feel different! Let it release if it needs to. What kind of sound do you want? Do you want to flip into falsetto or use your full voice?

> O'er the land of the free and the home of the brave?

The key to this is ending it with confidence and intention. After singing the high note, you don't want to end the piece without energy. So reduce your space but keep your intensity.

## HOMEWORK

Work on this piece and the ideas from this lesson in the coming days and weeks until you find your key and your most confident and expressive version. It is truly an accomplishment to sing this piece with confidence and ease!

# The Star-Spangled Banner
*(in A-flat Major)*

Music attributed to John Stafford
Smith Lyrics by Francis Scott Key

Arranged by
Dave & Peg Dunbar

**Maestoso** ♩ = 76

O— say, can you see, by the dawn's ear-ly light, what so proud-ly we hailed at the twi-light's last gleam-ing, whose broad stripes and bright stars, through the per-il-ous

© Arranged 2019 for The Great Courses by Dave & Peg Dunbar.

"The Star-Spangled Banner" in A-flat Major    [page 2]

fight, o'er the ram-parts we watched, were so gal-lant-ly stream-ing? And the rock-ets' red glare, the bombs burst-ing in air, gave proof through the night that our flag was still there. O say, does that star-spang-led ban-ner yet wave o'er the land of the free and the home of the brave?

© Arranged 2019 for The Great Courses by Dave & Peg Dunbar.

# The Star-Spangled Banner
*(in A Major)*

Music attributed to John Stafford
Smith Lyrics by Francis Scott Key

Arranged by
Dave & Peg Dunbar

**Maestoso** ♩ = 76

O say, can you see, by the dawn's ear-ly light, what so proud-ly we hailed at the twi-light's last gleam-ing, whose broad stripes and bright stars, through the per-il-ous

© Arranged 2019 for The Great Courses by Dave & Peg Dunbar.

"The Star-Spangled Banner" in A Major    [page 2]

fight, o'er the ram-parts we watched, were so gal-lant-ly stream-ing? And the rock-ets' red glare, the bombs burst-ing in air, gave proof through the night that our flag was still there. O say, does that star-spang-led ban-ner yet wave o'er the land of the free and the home of the brave?

© Arranged 2019 for The Great Courses by Dave & Peg Dunbar.

# The Star-Spangled Banner
*(in B-flat Major)*

Music attributed to John Stafford Smith Lyrics by Francis Scott Key

Arranged by Dave & Peg Dunbar

**Maestoso** ♩ = 76

O__ say, can you see, by the dawn's ear-ly light, what so proud-ly we hailed at the twi-light's last gleam-ing, whose broad stripes and bright stars, through the per-il-ous

© Arranged 2019 for The Great Courses by Dave & Peg Dunbar.

"The Star-Spangled Banner" in B-flat Major   [page 2]

# The Star-Spangled Banner
*(in B Major)*

Music attributed to John Stafford
Smith Lyrics by Francis Scott Key

Arranged by
Dave & Peg Dunbar

"The Star-Spangled Banner" in B Major   [page 2]

# LESSON 17
## *Training Your Tongue*

**FEATURED SONG**

"Ash Grove"

**EQUIPMENT NEEDED FOR VIDEO EXERCISES**

- straw
- mirror
- glass of water
- cloth or gauze pad or handheld massager

**LIST OF VIDEO EXERCISES**

- **EXERCISE 1:** Checking In with the Tongue
- **EXERCISE 2:** Tongue Sirens
- **EXERCISE 3:** "Ash Grove" Vowel Variations
- **EXERCISE 4:** Releasing the Larynx
- **EXERCISE 5:** Bite Your Tongue
- **EXERCISE 6:** Holding a Straw
- **EXERCISE 7:** "Ash Grove" Gargle
- **EXERCISE 8:** "Ash Grove" on a Nasal Consonant
- **EXERCISE 9:** "Ash Grove" on a Trill
- **EXERCISE 10:** Turkey and Reverse Turkey

The tongue is one of the most important articulators—and is by far the most active one—that humans have for speech and singing. It modifies the shape and characteristics of many cavities that impact the sounds you make, especially the oral cavity. It is a complicated organ made up of eight main muscles that make it strong and flexible. The tongue is also impressive in its endurance. Have you ever noticed how rarely your tongue gets tired?

# The Muscles of the Tongue

In addition to being a muscular organ, the tongue is covered with a moist mucosa and thousands of taste buds. It has a rough texture. Note that your taste buds aren't visible to the naked eye; the tiny bumps you can see are called papillae. The number of taste buds differs from person to person, and they are replaced about every two weeks.

Under the front of your tongue, connecting it to the bottom of your mouth, is the frenulum linguae. At the back, the tongue is anchored to the hyoid bone.

The tongue's eight muscles include four intrinsic and four extrinsic muscles. The intrinsic muscles change the shape of the tongue while the extrinsic ones change the position. The two main muscles we'll focus on in this lesson are extrinsic muscles: the genioglossus, which is the muscle that you use to stick out your tongue and is the only muscle that propels the tongue forward; and the hyoglossus, the muscle used to retract and depress the tongue.

The ability to use the muscles of the tongue for singing is important. Unfortunately, it is also one of the most common areas where negative tension occurs among vocal students. Generally, depressing and retracting are the most common detrimental tongue patterns. In other words, the hyoglossus is overactive. Because the hyoglossus originates in the hyoid bone, which is where the larynx is connected, it can put pressure down on the larynx, which is not advantageous to singing. Think of it like a damper pedal on a piano. If the tongue pushes against the larynx, it can deaden the vibration.

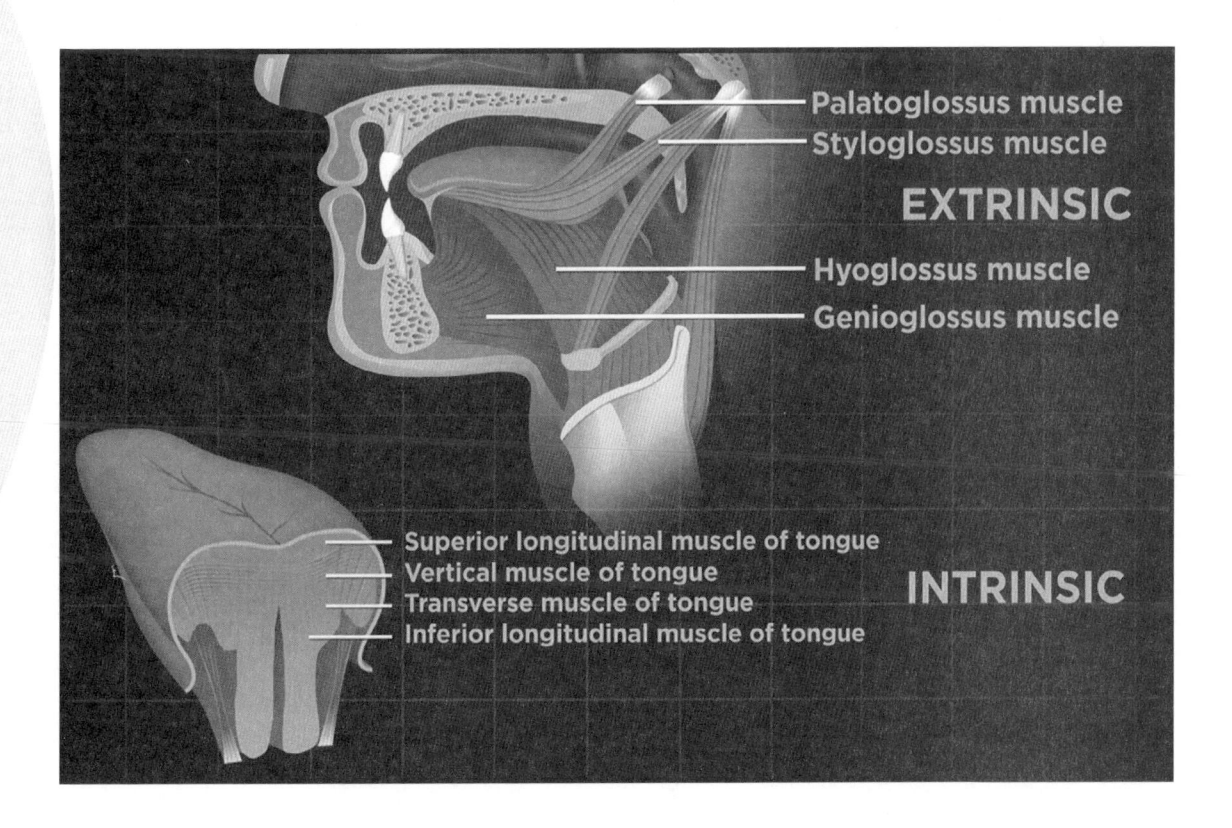

**EXTRINSIC**
- Palatoglossus muscle
- Styloglossus muscle
- Hyoglossus muscle
- Genioglossus muscle

**INTRINSIC**
- Superior longitudinal muscle of tongue
- Vertical muscle of tongue
- Transverse muscle of tongue
- Inferior longitudinal muscle of tongue

Tongue tension can manifest in many different ways. For example, when singers' jaws move up and down as they are singing, it is usually a result of tongue tension. When the tongue and jaw aren't working with good coordination, the muscles can get confused and constricted. Over time, this will cause fatigue and potential harm.

*Despite what you might have heard, the tongue is not the strongest muscle in the body.*

## Checking in with Your Tongue

Because the tongue can be such an issue, this lesson's video is packed with exercises. Don't feel like you need to master them all right now; they are tools that you can take out and work with when you want to.

All of the tongue exercises will take time to master, but you can make progress over time. In the same way that some people already have the flexibility to touch their toes and others need to work daily to improve their range of motion to be able to touch their toes, it might take time for you to be able to maintain release in the back of the tongue, or hyoglossus.

Start by checking in with your tongue. Gently take your thumbs and feel under your chin between the jawbone and the larynx. You are touching the underside of your tongue. It should feel soft and pliable.

Next, take a few breaths in and out to see if anything changes. You want everything to remain calm. If you feel any engagement pushing out or down, see if you can release it on the next breath.

With your hands, open your jaw slightly and take a few breaths through your mouth. Does this change anything? Again, release any engagement. You don't need your tongue muscles to breathe.

Next, give your tongue a little stretch. Stick it all the way out and relax your jaw. Now move the tongue over to the right, then to the left, and then up and down. Make a few big circles in both directions. Repeat this pattern a few times.

Now grab a cloth or gauze pad. Stick your tongue out and then use the cloth to grab it with your hands and give it a gentle tug, holding this position for about 30 seconds. Release and repeat a few more times.

Now massage under the chin while protruding and protracting the tongue, seeing if you can maintain calmness and avoid the bulge under your chin. You can use your thumbs, fingers, or knuckles or a handheld massager. See how much release you can find.

Next, open your mouth, put the tip of the tongue behind the teeth on the lower gum ridge. Allow the middle of the tongue to roll forward. Be sure to avoid shifting the jaw forward. Place one finger on your chin to monitor the jaw. Repeat this several times.

Now close your mouth, put just a pinky finger's width of space between your teeth, and do the same movement. It can be smaller but should generally feel the same. Can you feel a gentle curling? Repeat this movement several times. If you feel like you've forgotten how to find the curl, return to the open-mouth version and then start over.

Keep this internal space, noting the narrow space between your tongue and the top of your mouth. See if you can keep this space and feel the vibrations against the front teeth while you sing. Can your tongue stay in this easy arch? Are you tempted to pull back or lose the arch as you breathe or think about making sound? If so, return to the open-mouth version, then internalize, and finally add sound.

Remember that it is critical to engage in your beautifully developed cervical posture and use your understanding of your breath. So often the tensions in the tongue and the jaw come from compensations for a lack of breath connection, so everything you've done so far is critical for success here.

## Practicing with Internal Space

Now sing this lesson's song: "Ash Grove." How is your voice feeling?

Next, sing it on [i] with a slightly slower tempo, thinking about that internal, gently arched space.

Then, try this: Take the tip of your pinky finger and place it between your front teeth and sing the whole song on [i] with the tip of your tongue touching your pinky.

How was that? Many singers find [i] to be a wonderful forward vowel to vocalize on.

Next, alternate [i] and [ɑ]. Can you still maintain the connection with your pinky?

Are you noticing any pulling back, or is this pretty comfortable for you?

Now try singing the song with words again, maintaining awareness of the gentle motions of the tongue.

You can also do lip-tongue trills and tongue trills to release the tongue. Choose your favorite and sing through "Ash Grove" that way.

Finally, sing the song normally (with text and from the top) with the beautiful release you've been working on in this lesson.

# Ash Grove

Traditional Welsh folk song
Lyrics by Thomas Oliphant

Arranged by
Dave & Peg Dunbar

**Allegretto** ♩ = 116

Down yon-der green / Still glows the bright val-ley where stream-lets me-an-der, when twi-light is fad-ing I / sun-shine o'er val-ley and moun-tain, still war-bles the black-bird it's pen-sive-ly rove, or at the bright noon-tide in sol-i-tude / note from the tree; still trem-bles the moon-beam on stream-let and wan-der a-mid the dark shades of the lone-ly ash grove. 'Twas / foun-tain, but what are the beau-ties of na-ture to me? With

© Arranged 2019 for The Great Courses by Dave & Peg Dunbar.

"Ash Grove"  [page 2]

# LESSON 18

# *Articulating Vowels*

**FEATURED SONG**

"Awake! Awake!"

**EQUIPMENT NEEDED FOR VIDEO EXERCISES**

none

**LIST OF VIDEO EXERCISES**

- **EXERCISE 1**: Five Basic Vowels
- **EXERCISE 2**: High and Low Vowels
- **EXERCISE 3**: Lip Vowels

Diction, breath management, and beautiful tone are closely interwoven. In fact, when talking about the articulatory system, even in reference to pronunciation, we cannot truly separate this system from the other systems involved in singing. All of our systems coordinate together to create beautiful sound. This lesson focuses specifically on vowel production in singing.

# Articulation and Diction

One of the things that sets singers apart from other musicians is the use of language. Engagement with and delivery of text is a large part of the art form. Studying diction and articulation is a necessary and important element in the pursuit of beautiful singing.

Articulation is an adjustment to the shape and acoustic properties of the vocal tract. Your primary articulators are located in your facial skeleton, mandible, and cervical vertebrae. The ones that might come to mind right away are the lips, the tongue, and the teeth.

These are important, but remember that the muscles of the jaw, pharynx, palate, larynx, face, and head join these to form the complex and amazing system for articulation. Because many of the muscles of articulation serve several functions, one area can affect another easily. Learning to separate and clarify functions can help you maximize your vocal freedom and flexibility.

Speaking and singing have many things in common but are not exactly the same. Both speaking and singing use the breath, phonation, and articulation. Understanding how articulation in singing differs from speech will provide you with ways to make your diction more supportive of beautiful singing.

For example, when we are speaking, we tend to use our jaw a lot, but this is not advantageous for singing. While jaw movement is certainly used in diction in general, while singing, you want to be more efficient and specific with the use of the jaw. Because many of the muscles associated with the jaw connect to the hyoid bone at the front of the larynx, too much movement, tension, or misaligned positions of the jaw can put pressure on the larynx, resulting in constriction in the vocal cords.

Perhaps the most surprising reality about diction in singing is that jaw movement is not required for any of the vowels. Releasing jaw engagement and tension from your vowels can help to release the tension from your singing. This lesson focuses on engaging the most effective and efficient vowel production. It integrates all the tools developed in lesson 14 to release jaw tension while creating specific vowels with the tongue and lips.

The sounds identified as vowels are made up of the acoustic properties of all the resonating chambers between your vocal cords to your lips. Successful pronunciation requires subtle adjustments of the lips, tongue, soft palate, and jaw. Sound is affected by any small movement of these articulators.

*The articulatory, resonatory, and respiratory systems are hard to separate, as they are all intertwined.*

Vowels are important to singing because they render the most unhindered, consistent flow of breath where the vocal cords are in vibration. This same resonance path determines many other things about your tone—color, vibrancy, and quality.

It is important to recognize that the jaw, tongue, and lips all can move independently and have different functions when it comes to singing. Vowels can be categorized into tongue and lip vowels, but not jaw vowels. It's not that you don't move the jaw at all in your singing or in sound production, but you have a lot of flexibility beyond your jaw.

*Did you know that your lips are like a fingerprint? No two lips have identical impressions!*

## The International Phonetic Alphabet

One tool that singers use regularly is the International Phonetic Alphabet (IPA), which is a system of symbols that represent speech sounds. It was devised by linguists in the 19th century to create a standardized representation of the sounds used in spoken language.

In the IPA system, single symbols represent single sounds. It's useful for you to learn some basic IPA symbols to equip you with tools to communicate about vowels. In addition, learning the IPA will offer you the ability to use lots of resources that assist singers with articulation in any language. It's extremely beneficial for vocal students to translate a song's text into the IPA, even when singing in their native language. Getting specific about what vowels you are singing allows for optimum positions and resonance.

The IPA is a brilliant tool in the study of sound production, but the precise pronunciation in fine-tuning language skills is developed over time with the study of native inflection.

Most phoneticists classify vowels in three groups: frontal, central, and back. These classifications generally refer to the position of the tongue. In singing diction, vowels are often referred to as tongue or lip vowels. Perhaps the reason that the frontal, central, and back classifications are sometimes avoided with singing is because those terms can get confused with resonance and phonation classifications.

# The International Phonetic Alphabet
(revised to 2018)

## CONSONANTS (PULMONIC)

© 2018 IPA

|  | Bilabial | Labiodental | Dental | Alveolar | Postalveolar | Retroflex | Palatal | Velar | Uvular | Pharyngeal | Glottal |
|---|---|---|---|---|---|---|---|---|---|---|---|
| Plosive | p b |  |  | t d |  | ʈ ɖ | c ɟ | k g | q ɢ |  | ʔ |
| Nasal |  m |  ɱ |  | n |  | ɳ | ɲ | ŋ | ɴ |  |  |
| Trill |  ʙ |  |  | r |  |  |  |  | ʀ |  |  |
| Tap or Flap |  | ⱱ |  | ɾ |  | ɽ |  |  |  |  |  |
| Fricative | ɸ β | f v | θ ð | s z | ʃ ʒ | ʂ ʐ | ç ʝ | x ɣ | χ ʁ | ħ ʕ | h ɦ |
| Lateral fricative |  |  |  | ɬ ɮ |  |  |  |  |  |  |  |
| Approximant |  | ʋ |  | ɹ |  | ɻ | j | ɰ |  |  |  |
| Lateral approximant |  |  |  | l |  | ɭ | ʎ | ʟ |  |  |  |

Symbols to the right in a cell are voiced, to the left are voiceless. Shaded areas denote articulations judged impossible.

## CONSONANTS (NON-PULMONIC)

| Clicks | Voiced implosives | Ejectives |
|---|---|---|
| ʘ Bilabial | ɓ Bilabial | ʼ Examples: |
| ǀ Dental | ɗ Dental/alveolar | pʼ Bilabial |
| ǃ (Post)alveolar | ʄ Palatal | tʼ Dental/alveolar |
| ǂ Palatoalveolar | ɠ Velar | kʼ Velar |
| ǁ Alveolar lateral | ʛ Uvular | sʼ Alveolar fricative |

## OTHER SYMBOLS

ʍ Voiceless labial-velar fricative
w Voiced labial-velar approximant
ɥ Voiced labial-palatal approximant
ʜ Voiceless epiglottal fricative
ʢ Voiced epiglottal fricative
ʡ Epiglottal plosive

ɕ ʑ Alveolo-palatal fricatives
ɺ Voiced alveolar lateral flap
ɧ Simultaneous ʃ and x

Affricates and double articulations can be represented by two symbols joined by a tie bar if necessary.  t͡s k͡p

## VOWELS

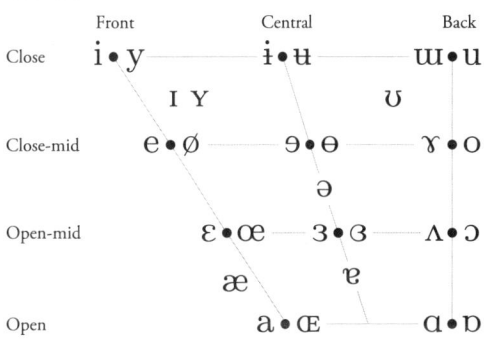

Front    Central    Back
Close    i•y    ɨ•ʉ    ɯ•u
         ɪ Y          ʊ
Close-mid e•ø    ɘ•ɵ    ɤ•o
                 ə
Open-mid ɛ•œ    ɜ•ɞ    ʌ•ɔ
         æ       ɐ
Open     a•ɶ         ɑ•ɒ

Where symbols appear in pairs, the one to the right represents a rounded vowel.

## SUPRASEGMENTALS

ˈ Primary stress          ˌfoʊnəˈtɪʃən
ˌ Secondary stress
ː Long                    eː
ˑ Half-long               eˑ
˘ Extra-short             ĕ
| Minor (foot) group
‖ Major (intonation) group
. Syllable break          ɹi.ækt
‿ Linking (absence of a break)

## DIACRITICS  Some diacritics may be placed above a symbol with a descender, e.g. ŋ̊

| ̥ | Voiceless | n̥ d̥ | ̤ | Breathy voiced | b̤ a̤ | ̪ | Dental | t̪ d̪ |
| ̬ | Voiced | s̬ t̬ | ̰ | Creaky voiced | b̰ a̰ | ̺ | Apical | t̺ d̺ |
| ʰ | Aspirated | tʰ dʰ | ̼ | Linguolabial | t̼ d̼ | ̻ | Laminal | t̻ d̻ |
| ̹ | More rounded | ɔ̹ | ʷ | Labialized | tʷ dʷ | ̃ | Nasalized | ẽ |
| ̜ | Less rounded | ɔ̜ | ʲ | Palatalized | tʲ dʲ | ⁿ | Nasal release | dⁿ |
| ̟ | Advanced | u̟ | ˠ | Velarized | tˠ dˠ | ˡ | Lateral release | dˡ |
| ̠ | Retracted | e̠ | ˤ | Pharyngealized | tˤ dˤ | ̚ | No audible release | d̚ |
| ̈ | Centralized | ë | ̴ | Velarized or pharyngealized | ɫ |
| ̽ | Mid-centralized | ẽ | ̝ | Raised | e̝ ( ɹ̝ = voiced alveolar fricative) |
| ̩ | Syllabic | n̩ | ̞ | Lowered | e̞ ( β̞ = voiced bilabial approximant) |
| ̯ | Non-syllabic | e̯ | ̘ | Advanced Tongue Root | e̘ |
| ˞ | Rhoticity | ɚ ɑ˞ | ̙ | Retracted Tongue Root | e̙ |

## TONES AND WORD ACCENTS

LEVEL                CONTOUR
ő or ˥ Extra high    ě or ˩˥ Rising
é  ˦ High            ê ˥˩ Falling
ē  ˧ Mid             ᷄ ˦˥ High rising
è  ˨ Low             ᷅ ˩˨ Low rising
ȅ  ˩ Extra low       ᷈ ˧˦˧ Rising-falling
↓ Downstep           ↗ Global rise
↑ Upstep             ↘ Global fall

# Types of Vowels in Singing

Remember that the tongue is comprised of eight muscles and is one of the muscular organs with the most endurance in the body. It is the primary tool that's used for creating speech. Generally, the resting position for the tongue is with the tip of the tongue behind the front teeth. The shape of the middle of the tongue plays a critical role in determining which harmonics are accentuated and therefore which vowel is perceived.

The following are some American English words that contain tongue vowels, moving from a high to low tongue position. Say the word first and then just the vowel.

    Heat – [i]
    Hit – [ɪ]
    Head – [ɛ]
    Hot – [ɑ]

The tip of the tongue remains behind the front teeth for every vowel; it is the height of the middle of the tongue that creates vowel shape. Remembering that the jaw doesn't create the vowel, try to make these vowel sounds and feel your tongue position. Look in the mirror for even more information. Use one finger to discourage jaw movement and work for maximum clarity of vowel and tone.

Lip vowels are often perceived as darker in vocal color. This happens because when the lips come forward, the vocal tract becomes longer and the pitch of the air is perceived as darker. Your lips are controlled by many facial muscles, from the chin up through the nose and even inside the cheeks. There are also more than 100 postural muscles that engage in some way to help you pucker your lips!

The irony of categorizing vowels as lip vowels is that in addition to the extraordinary coordination of the facial and postural muscles required to pucker the lips, these vowels also have specific tongue positions.

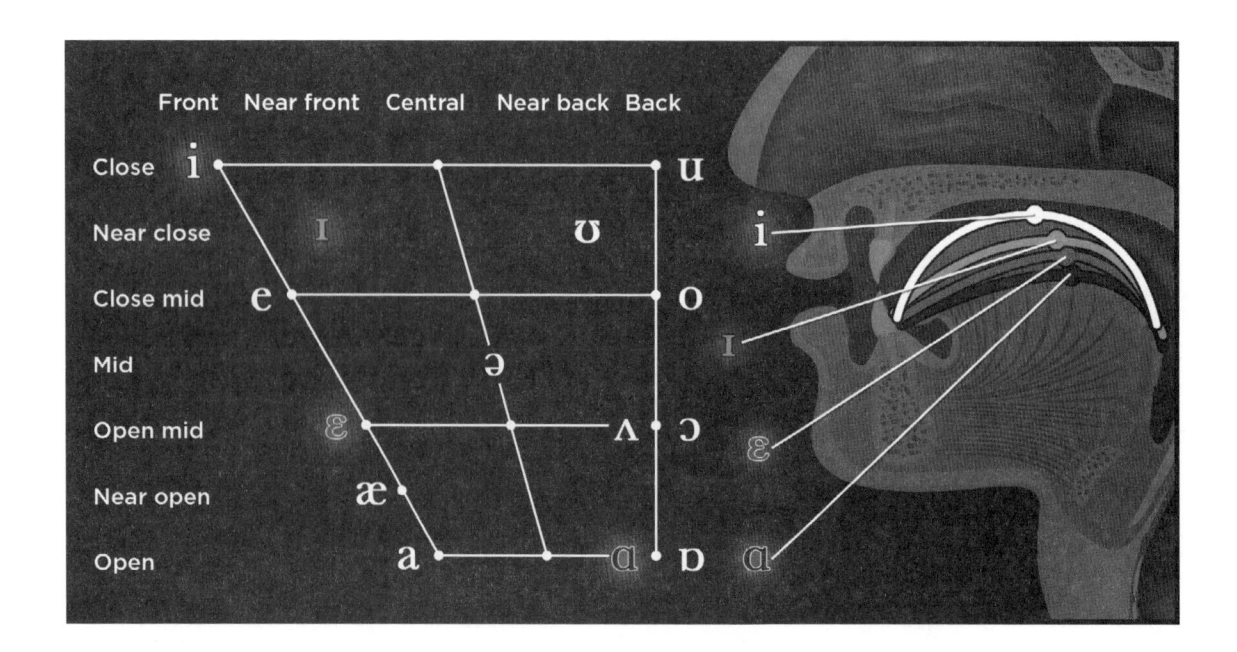

The following are some lip vowels. Say the word first and then just the vowel. The tip of the tongue remains behind the bottom front teeth while the lips round forward into a gentle pucker.

Boot – [u]
Boat – [o]
Book – [ʊ]
Bought – [ɔ]

In addition to tongue and lip vowels, there are other categories of vowels. One is called mixed vowels, which occur in English but are more prominent in other languages. These sounds are created by mixing the positions between the tongue and lip vowels.

There are also a few vowels that are referred to as neutral vowels. These vowels might be the most primitive and natural expression of sound that we use. We often use one when we are thinking of a response and need more time: "uhhh…." This vowel is notated like this in the IPA: [ʌ].

In singing, we frequently use the schwa, which is essentially the unaccented version of [ʌ]. We use it in the word *ocean*. Its symbol is [ə].

Another major thing that we encounter in the English language related to vowel production is diphthongs. A diphthong is a sound formed by the combination of two vowels in a single syllable. You start on one vowel and move toward another without the interruption of a consonant. In the IPA, a diphthong is notated with a symbol that looks like a colon but has triangles instead of dots and is placed between vowels (ː). Here are some examples; try to decode them.

1. [bɔːɪ] _____
2. [maːɪ] _____
3. [faːɪnd] _____
4. [seːɪ] _____
5. [laːʊd] _____

1. boy; 2. my; 3. find; 4. say; 5. loud

1. ˈpitər ˈpaːɪpər pɪkt ʌ pɛk ʌv ˈpɪkəld ˈpɛpərz
_____
_____

2. ʌ pɛk ʌv ˈpɪkəld ˈpɛpərz dɪd ˈpitər ˈpaːɪpər pɪk
_____
_____

3. ɪf ˈpitər ˈpaːɪpər pɪkt ʌ pɛk ʌv ˈpɪkəld ˈpɛpərz
_____
_____

4. wɛrz thʌ pɛk ʌv ˈpɪkəld ˈpɛpərz ˈpitər ˈpaːɪpər pɪkt
_____
_____

1. Peter Piper picked a peck of pickled peppers. 2. A peck of pickled peppers Peter Piper picked. 3. If Peter Piper picked a peck of pickled peppers. 4. Where's the peck of pickled peppers Peter Piper picked?

1. haːʊ mʌtʃ wʊd wʊd ʌ ˈwʊdtʃʌk tʃʌk
_____
_____

2. ɪf ʌ ˈwʊdtʃʌk kʊd tʃʌk wʊd?
_____
_____

3. hi wʊd tʃʌk, hi wʊd, æz mʌtʃ æz hi kʊd,
_____
_____

4. ænd tʃʌk æz mʊtʃ wʊd æz ʌ 'wʊdtʃʌk wʊd

_____

_____

5. ɪf ʌ 'wʊdtʃʌk kʊd tʃʌk wʊd.

_____

_____

> 1. How much wood would a woodchuck chuck
> 2. If a woodchuck could chuck wood?
> 3. He would chuck, he would, as much as he could,
> 4. And chuck as much wood as a woodchuck would
> 5. If a woodchuck could chuck wood.

# Practicing Vowel Articulation

Now it's time to analyze this lesson's piece: "Awake! Awake!" Think and speak through the song.

1. Awake! Awake! The hour is late!
2. Angels are knocking at your door!
3. They are in haste and cannot wait,
4. And once departed, come no more!

Can you put the vowels into the IPA?

1. _____
   _____

2. _____
   _____

3. _____
   _____

4. _____
   _____

Now sing the song slowly with attention to detail. Record yourself and see if you can hear diction through this lens.

Now play it back and listen carefully. Is there anything you'd like to alter or improve? Try singing the song again with your edits.

You can repeat the process of recording and listening at this tempo, making alterations as you go. Once you are happy with how you're singing the song, start to bring it up to tempo. You can do it gradually for the best retention.

Just like clarifying how your breath and phonation are working while singing, you will work to clarify and refine your diction.*

> 1. ə'weɪk! ə'weɪk! ðɪ 'aʊər ɪz leɪt!
> 2. 'eɪndʒəlz ɑr 'nɑkɪŋ æt jʊər dɔr!
> 3. ðeɪ ɑr ɪn heɪst ænd 'kænɑt weɪt,
> 4. ænd wʌns dɪˈpɑrtəd, kʌm noʊ mɔr!

---

\*   If you would like to learn more about the IPA, vowels, and diction rules, here are some resources:
    David Adams's *A Handbook of Diction for Singers*
    John Moriarty's *Diction*
    Joan Wall, Robert Caldwell, Tracy Gavilanes, and Sheila Allen's *Diction for Singers*

# Awake! Awake!

*(for one voice)*

Lyrics based on
"A Fragment" by Henry Wadsworth Longfellow

Music by
Dave & Peg Dunbar

**With great energy & bounce** ♩. = 90

A-wake! A-wake, the hour is late! An-gels are knock-ing at your door! They are in haste and can-not wait, and once de-part-ed come no more!

© Written 2019 for The Great Courses by Dave & Peg Dunbar.

# Awake! Awake!

(for three voices)*

Lyrics based on
"A Fragment" by Henry Wadsworth Longfellow

Music by
Dave & Peg Dunbar

*With great energy & bounce* ♩. = 90

[Solo 1, Solo 2, Solo 3, Piano sheet music]

Solo 1: A-wake! A-wake, the hour is late! An-gels are knock-ing at your door! They are in haste and can-not wait, and

Solo 2: A-wake! A-wake, the hour is late! An-gels are knock-ing at your door! They

Solo 3: A-wake! A-wake, the hour is late!

\* This scoring format is just to show that the ditty can be sung as a two- or three-part round in any combination.

© Written 2019 for The Great Courses by Dave & Peg Dunbar.

"Awake! Awake!" (for three voices)   [page 2]

# LESSON 19

# *Articulating Consonants*

**FEATURED SONG**

"A Rainy Day"

**EQUIPMENT NEEDED FOR VIDEO EXERCISES**

- ❑ mirror

**LIST OF VIDEO EXERCISES**

- ❑ **EXERCISE 1**: Differentiating Voiced and Unvoiced Consonants
- ❑ **EXERCISE 2**: Separating Lip and Jaw Motion
- ❑ **EXERCISE 3**: Voiced and Unvoiced Stop Consonants
- ❑ **EXERCISE 4**: Differentiating Nasal Consonants
- ❑ **EXERCISE 5**: Tongue Twisters

Articulation and pronunciation are important in being understood while singing. Engaging with good diction—diction that's easily understood—is what helps you delineate words. It takes practice to engage in good diction while coordinating beautiful legato and a consistent resonant tone. This lesson focuses on engaging with consonants while singing. It dives into consonant classification to help you understand how consonants are formed.

# The Classification of Consonants

A consonant is a sound that is formed when vibration is interrupted through the vocal tract. Consonants are classified by where and how they are articulated or interrupted. Interruption can occur anywhere between the lips and the glottis, including the teeth, tongue, alveolar ridge, hard palate, and soft palate. You don't need to avoid consonants to achieve a beautiful legato; rather, let them serve the clarification and separation of vowels.

This lesson focuses on English consonants, but the general rules apply across all languages. English is a consonant-heavy language with somewhat equal distribution of vowels and consonants.

Consider the length of consonants. As you elongate speech by singing, in a language that values consonants, you want to give consonants more time rather than making them forceful or louder to accentuate them. English can certainly benefit from attention to the length of consonants.

Articulation is an adjustment to the shape and acoustic properties of the vocal tract. Your primary articulators are located in your facial skeleton, mandible, and cervical vertebrae. The ones that might come to mind are the lips, tongue, and teeth. These are certainly important, but remember that the muscles of the jaw, pharynx, palate, larynx, face, and head join these to form the complex and amazing system that forms articulation.

Remember that many of the muscles of articulation serve several functions. One area can affect another easily. Learning to separate and clarify functions can help you maximize your vocal freedom and flexibility.

Linguists have developed a consonant classification chart that serves a similar function to the vowel chart found in the previous lesson. The purpose of a consonant classification chart is to explain where in the mouth different consonant sounds are produced and how the air and vibration engage with the tone to create individual sounds. The chart on the following page shows where the sound is produced across the top and how it is produced down the side.

# Where Sounds Are Produced

You've already learned a lot about the anatomy of your vocal mechanism; that will support the understanding of creating diction-specific language.

- **Bilabial** consonants use both lips.

- **Labiodental** consonants use the lower lip and upper teeth.

- **Dental** consonants are created between the teeth and tongue.

- **Alveolar** consonants are created with the tongue and the ridge behind the upper teeth.

- **Postalveolar** consonants are articulated behind the alveolar consonants, with the tongue near or touching the back of the alveolar ridge but a bit farther back.

- **Palatal** consonants use the tongue and the hard palate.

- **Velar** consonants are made using the soft palate in the back of the mouth.

- **Glottal** consonants are created in the throat between the vocal cords.

## CONSONANT CLASSIFICATION CHART

| | | | \multicolumn{8}{c}{PLACE} |
|---|---|---|---|---|---|---|---|---|---|---|
| | | | \multicolumn{2}{c}{LABIAL} | \multicolumn{4}{c}{CORONAL} | \multicolumn{2}{c}{DORSAL} |
| | MANNER | VOICING | Bilabial | Labiodental | Dental | Alveolar | Postalveolar | Palatal | Velar | Glottal |
| **OBSTRUENTS** | Stop | Voiceless | p | | | t | | | k | |
| | | Voiced | b | | | d | | | g | |
| | Fricative | Voiceless | | f | θ * | s | ʃ ‡ | | | h |
| | | Voiced | | v | ð † | z | ʒ § | | | |
| | Affricate | Voiceless | | | | | tʃ ¶ | | | |
| | | Voiced | | | | | dʒ ** | | | |
| **SONORANTS** | Nasal | Voiced | m | | | n | | | ŋ ‡‡ | |
| | Liquid — Lateral | Voiced | | | | l | | | | |
| | Liquid — Rhotic | Voiced | | | | ɹ †† | | | | |
| | Glide | Voiced | w | | | | | j | w | |

\* [θ] (the *th-* sound in *through*); † [ð] (the *th-* sound in *that*); ‡ [ʃ] (the *sh-* sound in *shoe*); § [ʒ] (the *-ge* sound in *beige*); ¶ [tʃ] (the *ch-* sound in *chug*); ** [dʒ] (the *j-* sound in *jug*); †† [ɹ] (the standard English *r* sound); ‡‡ [ŋ] (the *-ng* sound in *sing*)

# How Sounds Are Articulated

Different variables are involved when producing sound, including tongue position, airflow, and whether it's voiced or unvoiced.

- **Stops** are created when air coming from the lungs is stopped at some point during the formation of the sound. These stops block the outward flow of air with an audible puff. Some of these sounds are unvoiced and others are voiced. Voiced consonants use tone while unvoiced are created with only breath—no phonation.§§

- **Fricatives** occur when restricted airflow causes friction but the airflow isn't completely stopped. The airstream passes through a constriction somewhere along the vocal tract, and the friction causes air to become turbulent.¶¶

- **Affricates** are combinations of stops and fricatives.

- With **nasal** consonants, the air is stopped from going through the mouth by a dropped palate and is redirected into the nose.

- With **liquid** consonants, almost no air is stopped.

- **Glides** are sometimes referred to as semivowels. The air passes through the articulators to create vowellike sounds, but the letters are known as consonants.

Note that you don't have to phonate at all to create the unvoiced sounds—there are no vocal fold vibrations. This can be confusing while singing, especially because there are often voiced and unvoiced versions of the same mouth position. For example, consider the bilabial stop [p], which is unvoiced, and [b], which is voiced.

Most of this will come naturally to you, but while singing, it is nice to know how sounds are formed so that you can address issues that might arise with the unique challenge of sustained tone.

---

§§ The following are examples of unvoiced consonants: [p], [t] and [k]. These are the voiced versions: [b], [d], and [g].

¶¶ The following are unvoiced: [f], [θ], [s], [ʃ], and [h]. These are the voiced versions: [v], [ð], [z], and [ʒ].

# Practicing Consonant Articulation

Tongue twisters can help you exercise your articulators for better diction. You can make up one on your own or try this one: Many mumbling mice are making merry music in the moonlight. Mighty nice!

Take a moment to think through the text of this lesson's song, "A Rainy Day," with the lens of consonant articulation.

First, speak the text. Then, intonate it slowly so that you can discover what challenges might lead to a less-than-beautiful tone.

> Oh, what a blessed interval
> A rainy day may be!
> No lightning flash nor tempest roar,
> But one incessant, steady pour
> Of dripping melody;
> A rainy day can be a blessed interval!
> A little halt for introspect,
> A little moment to reflect,
> With life, a chance to reconnect,
> A virtual symphony!

In general, anticipating consonants—putting them before the beat—can help elongate the vowel and clarify the word. If you anticipate the consonant, the diction will be better understood, you will have more time for your vowel, and the harmonic structure of the music will be more apparent.

Now sing the song with the melody, paying special attention to voice and unvoiced consonants. You might want to record yourself or ask a friend to listen with an attentive ear.

**HOMEWORK**

Play with classifications. The reason it is helpful to understand these for singing is to clarify where in the mouth sounds occur. Sometimes when you engage in the intensity added to your sound by adding tone and sustain, it can be easy to blur your speech.

# A Rainy Day

Lyrics based on
"A Rainy Day" by Hattie Howard

Music by
Dave & Peg Dunbar

*Gently* ♩ = 64

Oh, what a bless-ed in-ter-val a rain-y day may be! No light-ning flash nor temp-est roar, but one in-ces-sant stead-y pour of drip-ping mel-od-y. A rain-y day can be a bless-ed in-ter-val: A lit-tle halt for in-tro-spect, a lit-tle mom-ent to ref-lect, with life, a chance to re-con-nect, a vir-tual sym-phon-y!

© Written 2019 for The Great Courses by Dave & Peg Dunbar.

# LESSON 20
# Diction for Singing

**FEATURED SONG**

"Our Garden"

**EQUIPMENT NEEDED FOR VIDEO EXERCISES**

none

**LIST OF VIDEO EXERCISES**

- ❑ **EXERCISE 1:** Resonance Balancing

Beyond articulation is pronunciation. In addition to forming the shapes of sound with your vocal mechanism, you will need to select which sounds to add syllabic stress to by using length, pitch, and volume.

# Word Stress

Generally, the words of any language will have strong and weak syllables that help us recognize the words' meanings. There are several words in English that can change meaning depending on where you put the stress, such as *present, produce, conduct*, and *recall*. (For example, compare these two pronunciations and uses of *recall*: A recall was issued on my baby stroller last week; I can't recall what I ate yesterday afternoon.)

It is fairly easy to speak these words with the stress that's correct for the context. But try to sing them—both versions of each of the words just mentioned—to discover some potential challenges and tools for addressing them while singing. Because you don't determine duration, rhythm, or pitch while singing in the same way you do when you speak, you'll need to use your singer tools to pronounce words with care.

This lesson's song, "Our Garden," has a lot of even rhythms without much natural word stress.

First, try singing "Our Garden" under tempo, with equally distributed articulation, minus word stress. It is advantageous to try it slowly first to get it down on the breath and the voice before you take it up to full tempo. This is a good way to practice with any fast piece. When you try to go too fast too soon, you end up using less breath and space than you have available to you and sometimes skip over many of the tools you've learned so far.

Once this becomes comfortable, try singing the song at tempo this way, still without the word stress.

When you remove the ebb and flow and flexibility of the language that you are accustomed to, you lose some agility and flexibility in the voice. This time, allow—or perhaps even encourage—the ebb and flow of language. Do the slow version first and then bring it up to tempo.

In addition to syllabic stress, you want to think about how words should be stressed relative to each other within the phrase. What words do you want to bring out as important?

When you want to figure out the best phrasing, speak the line first and make some choices. On your music, underline the words you decide you want to bring out. This is where artistry starts to come into play. There is no right answer. You want to consider the poetry and what the composer tells you about where he or she wants the word stress—but in the end, you make your own decision.

One important thing to remember while deciding on phrasing is that a rest does not mean that you have to break phrases or take an inhalation. Remember that you want to evoke your natural human rhythm. When you speak, you do not always inhale between every thought or every sentence. You breathe when you need to or perhaps in response to something. You definitely won't want to inhale between every rest in this piece or you'll stack the breath or maybe even hyperventilate!

Here's one way you could emphasize the following text from "Our Garden"; the underlined words are the ones that are emphasized.

We have a little garden of our <u>own</u>.
And ev'ry day we water there the seeds that <u>we</u> have sown.
We tend our little garden with <u>such</u> care,
You <u>won't</u> find a <u>faded</u> leaf nor a <u>blighted</u> blossom there.
You won't find a faded leaf nor a blighted blossom <u>there</u>.

# Diction as a Tool

Normally, when you are singing in your native language, it can be helpful to use a dictionary for correct diction in singing just as you would if you were singing in a foreign language.

For example, consider the word *talk*. When you are speaking, the details of the word are less noticeable, but when you slow down and sustain words on pitch, these details matter. We don't pronounce the *l* even though that's how it's spelled. This becomes important when you start to elongate text.

In "Our Garden," note that the composer chose to clarify the syllabification of *every* by removing the middle syllable (*ev'ry*). This tells you that the composer wants you to speak it with only two syllables. If you look up the word in the dictionary, you'll find that that's how it is intended to be pronounced. However, you have surely heard some people say *ev-er-y*, and some composers set the word this way. You can take *ev'ry* as an indication that the composer of this piece is looking for pure and natural diction.

Our regional accents can creep into our singing if we allow them to. Singers tend to avoid accentuating their own regionalism in many singing styles. Recognize that eliminating your regionalism as a habit in singing allows freedom to use diction as a means of expression and styling. For styles where you do want to accentuate your regional accent, understanding what you are doing with the language that brings across the accent and style is critical.

In this lesson, focus on pronouncing the text purely—free of regional accents. Use the English dictionary pronunciations throughout the piece.

In English, there are a lot of diphthongs, or a blending of two vowels spoken in the same syllable. The syllable is initiated to create one vowel and smoothly transitions to the position for another vowel. This is another thing you can use as an expression and styling tool. Generally, you elongate the accented part of the diphthong. For example, the words *own*, *sown*, *care*, *there*, and *blighted* are words to acknowledge the diphthongs. Now sing through "Our Garden" slowly and pay special attention to the diphthongs.

In general, something to watch for while singing is vowel contaminators: sounds that are categorized as either nasal or liquid voiced consonants. They can easily be sustained while singing, but you have to be careful not to let them replace the vowel while sustaining tone. Examples of vowel contaminators are *n*, *ng*, *m*, *l*, and *r*.

Just look at the title of the piece: "Our Garden." Using *r* and *n* as if they were vowels will create a specific sound that doesn't look like the dictionary version of the word that you are looking for.

Speak through the text and identify moments that you may have to pay attention to. Specifically look at *n*, *m*, and *ng*.

In English, *r* is not a vowel, but we sometimes treat it like one. In the song title "Our Garden," the *r* could easily be treated like a vowel in *Our* and in *Garden*. While singing, especially in the classical style, we generally sing a schwa ([ə], as in the *ea* in *ocean*) to represent the sustained [r]. There are styles where you might choose to lean into the liquid [r], but in general, know that you can make it more comfortable by using the schwa.

You can practice this skill with "Our Garden." Sing the third line of "Our Garden" and sustain the final syllable.

> We tend our little garden with such care

Can you find a sustained *r* that doesn't put a ton of extra tension on your mechanism? You can pucker your lips slightly to encourage a longer vocal tract with a slight stabilization in the larynx. It also rounds and mixes the sound to move toward the schwa vowel and releases some of the temptation to use the jaw.

Another example of a consonant we often treat as a vowel in English is *l*. There are a few ways to produce the [l] sound. Say "a lot" and "a little."

Can you feel the difference? When the *l* is followed by an *i*, we are more likely to use a forward resonance, resisting the temptation to pull down on the larynx. In some languages, such as Russian, there are words where you truly must engage in the back *l* to differentiate two words. In English, you can practice using the forward *l* in order to minimize stress on the vocal mechanism while singing, despite the fact that in speaking, we do both.

Speak the first phrase of "Our Garden" slowly, first engaging the back *l*.

> We have a little garden of our own.

Then, sing it that way.

Next, speak the phrase, engaging the front *l*. Note how the front one puts less pressure and doesn't move your mechanism as much, allowing for an easier laryngeal stability. You don't even have to close your mouth between "a" and "li."

Now try singing it that way.

Diction can also help you stay in tempo with a fast song—like this lesson's song. In general, vowels go on the beat and consonants come slightly before the beat.

Try this with "Our Garden." First, take off the consonants and only sing on vowels so that you can feel what it is like to give each note its full value.

Then, insert consonants into that version, keeping the vowels long and anticipating beginning consonants and delaying final ones when you have time. You'll especially reap the benefits on the final sustained tones.

Can you feel the difference? Keep playing with this.

*Up until this point in the course, you have focused primarily on building your technical vocabulary as a singer. As you move forward, it is time to start using your tools to create art.*

*Bring your artist to the table and use intentional pronunciation to create your own meaningful version of "Our Garden." What does this text mean to you? What is your intention? Who are you talking to or singing with?*

# Our Garden

Lyrics based on
"A Garden" by Helen Beatrix Potter

Music by
Dave & Peg Dunbar

We have a lit-tle gar-den of our own, and ev-'ry-day we wat-er there the seeds that we have sown. We tend our lit-tle gar-den with such

© Written 2019 for The Great Courses by Dave & Peg Dunbar.

"Our Garden"   [page 2]

# LESSON 20—DICTION FOR SINGING

**THIS PAGE INTENTIONALLY LEFT BLANK.**

# LESSON 21
# *Engaging with Lyrics*

**FEATURED SONG**

"The Alarm Clock"

**EQUIPMENT NEEDED FOR VIDEO EXERCISES**

☐ character analysis worksheet

**LIST OF VIDEO EXERCISES**

none

There is one more step to address when it comes to text as you work toward being the best singing performer you can be. You now have tools to support beautiful posture, breath, tone, and diction. What are you going to do with all of that? Hopefully, you desire to communicate. When you have text, you need to learn how to approach and prepare to engage with text.

# Interpreting Text and Character

When you take on a role, you should go through the libretto carefully, as well as any source material that is available to you.

First, you have to do some research and make some decisions. Start by being informed about your poet and/or librettist. As you do this research, be sure to note if the work is based on a larger work or a real event. If it is, read the original work or learn more about the event. Note the time period and consider the historical context of the writing. Who is the writer and in what setting did he or she write the text? What does the librettist/poet say? Are there interviews, articles, or commentary that give insight into the work?

Next, find out more about your composer and the context in which he or she composed the work. Who was the composer and in what setting did he or she choose, commission, or write the text? Did the composer know the text writer? If not, how did the composer come by the text or story? Was the piece written for a specific audience or commissioned for an event? How was it received in the premiere? What does the composer say? Again, find commentary.

Note that the composer has already interpreted the text by setting it to music. The composer can give you a lot of information to work with based on how he or she set the text.

Character analysis is crucial if you are playing a role in an opera, an oratorio, or a musical. However, it is good to get specific about character and intention no matter what you are preparing to sing. If you are lucky enough to have information from the librettist or lyricist, or the composer, or other source material, you can use that, but if not, you'll use your imagination. Once you are confident in your research, you'll use the questions in the following character analysis worksheet to make informed decisions that give your performance depth and personality.

# Character Analysis Worksheet

Consider the following while preparing character: text, music, source material, historical context, and performance tradition. (Note that sometimes this information will be present in the score and sometimes you will need to use your informed imagination to create a well-rounded character.)

a. *Who am I (the character)?*

   (Consider gender, age, size, childhood, education, nationality, class, faith, look, family, occupation, energy level, walk, self-image, etc.)

   _____
   _____

b. *What does my physicality reveal?*

   (Consider posture, facial expression, gesture, eyes, mannerisms, size tempo, scope of gestures, etc.)

   _____
   _____

c. *Where am I?*

   (Consider a familiar or uncomfortable place, temperature, period, time of day, etc.)

   _____
   _____

d. *Who am I talking to?*

   (Consider relationship, power dynamic, length of familiarity, etc.)

   _____
   _____

e. *What is unique today?*

   (Is there a clear shift you want to indicate with a physical change?)

   _____
   _____

**f.** *What do I want?*

(What physical gestures/facial expressions communicate this?) What are the stakes?

_____
_____

**g.** *What are my expectations?*

_____
_____

**h.** *What are the obstacles?*

_____
_____

**i.** *What are my tactics?*

(Use action verbs.)

_____
_____

## BONUS QUESTIONS TO CONSIDER

**1.** How is this character similar to me? How do I relate to this character? How am I different?

_____
_____

**2.** What is my character's biggest secret?

_____
_____

**3.** What is my character's favorite fairy tale and why?

_____
_____

# Practicing Interpretation

This lesson's piece—"The Alarm Clock"—doesn't have a ton of information readily available about it, so you can focus on the creative part and see how that can influence your performance. Here's the text:

> With a clatter and a jangle,
> And a wrangle and a screech,
> How the old alarm clock wheezes
> As it sneezes out of reach!
> How you groan and yawn and stretch
> In the chilly morning air,
> As you pull the blankets tight,
> With your head clear out of sight—
> And you swear!

Do you feel a connection to this text? Have you felt this way? If you haven't, can you remember a time when you've seen this play out with a family member or friend or even a character on a TV show? How do you want to express this poetry?

Start with what you can learn about the poet, composer, and context.

This poem came from a book that Edwin Carty Ranck published in 1906 titled *Poems for Pale People*. The preface offers a bit of insight into Ranck's intention for this text. Here are a few sentences from him regarding his poems:

> This little volume was written for no reason on earth and with no earthly reason. It just simply happened, on the principle, I suppose that "murder will out." Murder is a bad thing and so are nonsense rhymes. There is often a valid excuse for murder; there is none for nonsense rhymes. … It really never pays to think. Thinking is too much like work. After reading these rhymes you will not think that the writer ever did think, which after all is the right way to think.

With your character in mind, think about your performance of this song. Is your character a morning person? Does your character often wake up before his or her alarm and try to find the softest, gentlest alarm clock available? Or does your character set an alarm for at least an hour before he or she needs to get up and press snooze a million times?

The "swearing" could be the actual getting up or perhaps giving in to going back to sleep—you get to choose! Perhaps you might take a different option for the final pitch based on whatever kind of "swearing" you choose.

What are your ideas? Who is your character? Use your imagination in combination with your tools to create your version of your music. The key is having a clear intention about what you would like to communicate.

Bring your unique self to every piece you approach and you will be effective in your communication and performance.

# The Alarm Clock

Lyrics from "The Alarm Clock" by
Edwin C. Ranck

Music by
Dave Dunbar

**A la Tarantella** ♩. = 110

With a clat-ter and a jan-gle, and a wrang-le and a screech, how the old al-arm clock wheez-es as it sneez-es out of reach! How you groan and yawn and stretch in the

© Written 2019 for The Great Courses by Dave Dunbar.

"The Alarm Clock"  [page 2]

# LESSON 22

# Communicating through Song

**FEATURED SONG**

"Auld Lang Syne"

**EQUIPMENT NEEDED FOR VIDEO EXERCISES**

- ❏ attitude cards

**LIST OF VIDEO EXERCISES**

- ❏ **EXERCISE 1**: Body Scan
- ❏ **EXERCISE 2**: Attitude Cards
- ❏ **EXERCISE 3**: Changing Attitudes

If you intend to take your singing to the level of performance, it will most likely involve facing an audience. In preparation for such an occasion, there are tools that you can use to develop your skills as a singing actor. This lesson focuses on the communication element of being a singer.

## Basic Tools for Performance

You are a great interpreter of song. Moving your intention through your technique for a successful delivery is an important step. But know that having true intentions isn't always enough! It is important as a performer that you learn to align your intentions with the message the audience is receiving. You want to get what you think you are expressing and what you are actually expressing to match.

The mirror and the video are your friends. If you want to see how you are being perceived, you should look at yourself from the outside.

Sing for a friend or colleague who you can present with specific questions about your intentions. You don't have to ask the person generally what he or she thinks; that might open a gate you might prefer to close. However, you can ask them specific questions like these: What intentions did you see in my performance? What message did you receive?

If you aren't already a natural actor, just know that—like learning to sing—learning to be a singing actor is very possible. Some will be naturally adept while others will need to take time to refine and develop their skills, but everyone can do it!

## Visual Methods of Expression

The tools you've learned in this course can be expressive as well as supportive of technical production of sound. And they all work together!

Start with body awareness—something you've been working on throughout this course. Take a moment to do a body scan. Are you engaging in tension anywhere that you can afford to release? Find the whole body in full connection and maintain that connection. You are working to have awareness of the body at the same time you are aware of your external space.

Posture is one area where you can express your intention, character, and state of mind. It is astounding how much our bodies can say without a single word. From a very early age, we learn to read and understand the physical messages that bodies send.

*A singer's instrument is the body—the self. You use the same mechanism to sing that you use to speak; the only difference is the dominant acoustic properties.*

The challenge with this is learning to balance postural needs. While you want to utilize your best posture as a singer, as a performer you might choose to alter your external posture to communicate the poetry more accurately. Once you've established what you need for singing well, you can layer it with so many more things.

Think about what your external posture communicates. What are the different messages that posture can send? This is something you will always want to consider both in relation to your singing and your song. What message is your posture sending? Be intentional about what you are communicating with your posture.

Another tool you have is facial expression. Don't forget your eyes and focus; these are a part of facial expression but also can exist and express devoid of other facial postures.

Another physical way of expressing is through gesture. Perhaps the most obvious places to engage with gesture are your arms and hands. Plan what you will do with your arms and hands while singing. Again, video or photograph yourself to see how your gestures are being read. Watch others and mimic to get a sense for what a particular gesture feels like in your own body. Do your best to create meaningful gestures that stem from the center of your body and consider what messages are sent with each gesture. Also consider your legs and feet. What does your stance, balance, and placement say?

Learning to gesture is just another skill. If you aren't sure what to do with your hands and arms, it just means that you need to practice, like anything else. You shouldn't expect that your gestures will magically show up on the day of your performance. Practice gesture right alongside your other skills. Again, feel free to video yourself to see if you're communicating what you think you are communicating. In most cases, there is no right or wrong. Just know that everything you do sends a message, and it is important to know what message you are sending.

## Nonvisual Methods of Expression

In addition to visible ways of expressing character—such as posture, facial expression, and gesture—there are ways to use the vocabulary you've developed in this course to deliver your message with your whole instrument.

How could you do that with breath? Perhaps you add an audible breath for expression or you breathe less or more often to communicate your intention. Be sure that your intention or thought happens before you breathe to sing. This is important for sincerity, as it is how we function as human beings. We have our thought before we take in air to express it: Think, breathe, express (in this case, through singing). Because of this, it is important to plan and practice your phrasing.

Experiment and find the breaths that best articulate your ideas and intention.

Now consider the text of this lesson's song, "Auld Lang Syne,"* and make some decisions about breath. Speak the text and find your phrasing. Try different breaths.

> Should old acquaintance be forgot and never brought to mind?
> Should old acquaintance be forgot and days of auld lang syne?
> For auld lang syne, my dear, for auld lang syne,
> We'll take a cup of kindness yet for auld lang syne.

This is a moment when your artistry gets to shine through. Each individual will have different perspectives and ideas about what and how to express themselves.

In addition to posture, facial expression, gesture, and breath, other tools you've learned are phonation and resonance choices. How would you like to utilize dynamics and vocal colors?

Imagine it's New Year's Eve. What kind of year have you had? What kind of year would you like to have next year? What if you were singing the song from the perspective of someone who is very angry with how the past year has gone. What is your most annoying sound? Perhaps it's nasal or very bright. Play with your most annoying sound for the first verse.

What if you have been having the best vacation ever and today is the last day. What vocal color might you choose? Perhaps you like to choose longing, using a high palate and lots of space.

Other tools you have in your toolbox are articulation and pronunciation. What kind of "Auld Lang Syne" do you want to share? What would you like to try? Play with articulation while singing the song.

Now do your character analysis for this song. It is often a group celebration piece and not a solo piece, but try to look at it through a different lens. Think about what you want to communicate. You can even be the character if you want to; just think through the full details and be mindful of what you present.

---

\* Traditionally sung on New Year's Eve, this piece is a poem written by Robert Burns in 1788. The melody comes from a traditional folk song. The phrase *auld lang syne* originated in the Scots language, which is a close cousin of English, and it roughly translates to "times gone by."

# Attitude Cards

Attitude cards are great tools for testing whether your intention is aligned with your presentation.

Record yourself saying this short phrase—"This is really big!"—with each of the following attitudes:

| | |
|---|---|
| furious | defiant |
| exultant | mournful |
| ashamed | wary |
| fierce | tender |
| reverent | frantic |
| inspired | sorrowful |
| joyful | confident |
| astonished | pleading |
| miserable | blissful |
| majestic | |

Now watch your recording. As you watch, write down what intentions you see and hear. Be honest! Perhaps watch the recording once without sound to make sure you aren't influenced by hearing the directed intention. Are there any areas you are more or less connected to?

Exploring attitudes is useful when working on aligning your desired result with your intention. Attitude cards can also be freeing when you're stuck in a one-dimensional interpretation of text.

Play with attitude cards on the first phrase of "Auld Lang Syne." Repeat each line of the song twice, trying a different attitude to see which one you prefer; suggested attitudes are given below. Again, this is a good time to record yourself. You are looking to see how your attitude aligns with your delivery.

**grieving**:
Should old acquaintance be forgot and never brought to mind?

**tentative**:
Should old acquaintance be forgot and never brought to mind?

**delighted**:
Should old acquaintance be forgot and auld lang syne?

**confident**:
Should old acquaintance be forgot and auld lang syne?

**bitterly**:
For auld lang syne, my dear, for auld lang syne,

**sweetly**:
For auld lang syne, my dear, for auld lang syne,

**hidden**:
We'll take a cup of kindness yet for auld lang syne.

**public**:
We'll take a cup of kindness yet for auld lang syne.

# Tactics

We can't stop at attitude. For example, we don't walk around deciding to act "furious"; the actions that demonstrate "furious" are just the result of a reaction or intention. So instead of using attitudes, we can break the text down with tactics.

Tactics are methods used to achieve goals. When we communicate, we are motivated by intention—we have objectives and obstacles. What do you want, and what is in the way? You might develop different tactics to approach the same problem should one tactic not work.

This process can be related to football. Your goal is to win, but the way that you achieve that goal is through different plays, or tactics. You might choose to pass on one play, but if it is blocked by the other team (this is your obstacle), you might try running a play next. It is this series of mini decisions that you engage with when you are performing.

Here are a few tactics to consider for "Auld Lang Syne," but just think of these as a jumping-off point and explore others, too:

| | |
|---|---|
| forgive | validate |
| admonish | warn |
| convince | resist |
| ignore | amuse |
| mislead | |

Set your own intention and decide on several tactics—at least four and perhaps up to 12 for "Auld Lang Syne." Then, sing while projecting your choices.

---

*Just look at all the tools and choices you have as a singer! Use your imagination in combination with your tools to create your version of your music. The key is having a clear intention about what you would like to communicate. Bring your unique self to every piece you approach and you will be effective in your communication and performance.*

# Auld Lang Syne

Music based on "Times Long Past," an English folk song
Lyrics by Robert Burns

Arranged by
Dave & Peg Dunbar

Should old acquaintance be forgot and never brought to mind? Should old acquaintance be forgot and days of auld lang syne? For auld lang syne, my dear, for

© Arranged 2019 for The Great Courses by Dave & Peg Dunbar.

"Auld Lang Syne"  [page 2]

# LESSON 23

# *Making Each Performance Personal*

**FEATURED SONG**

"Danny Boy"

**EQUIPMENT NEEDED FOR VIDEO EXERCISES**

none

**LIST OF VIDEO EXERCISES**

none

From the natural instinct to sing lullabies to a newborn baby to international events that lead us to unite our voices in song, we use our sounds to communicate. Singing is one the most powerful and universal ways to communicate.

# Communicating Your Unique Perspective

It takes courage to start using newly acquired tools to communicate through music in the same way that it takes courage to speak another language or even introduce new words into your native-language vocabulary.

Have you ever studied another language, felt good about your grasp on that language, and then visited the country of origin for that language? What felt proficient in the classroom perhaps felt inefficient when put into practice. Communicating complex ideas and thoughts with others who have mastered the language is a completely different feeling from classroom learning.

It takes deliberate practice and patience to feel ownership of a new language. Singing with your new technical language will take the same kind of practice and patience. Stick with it and it will pay off! Having solid vocal technique; learning the words, notes, and rhythms of your song; and studying the text of your music lays the foundation for effective communication.

Music is powerful as communication even without the voice or words. Imagine the possibilities when you add your unique voice and inspired text to music!

You are uniquely you. And when you sing, you have to be willing to share your unique perspective. First and foremost, you have your own imagination. You must believe what you are saying as you sing, just as you do when you speak, for it to be called communication. This is perhaps the most important thing about singing: It requires you to be vulnerable, honest, and intentional.

As humans, we can sense and feel when someone is communicating with sincerity and intention. But how can you be sincere in your message if you are singing about something you haven't experienced? For example, how can you sing about a specific place like Venice if you have not been there? You can look at pictures and videos of Venice and imagine what it would be like to be there. Even more specifically, how can you sing about a boat race in the canals of Venice if you've never seen a regatta? You can draw on your experiences to effectively use your imagination. You've likely seen car or human races, or been in a rowdy crowd cheering at events, or been in a rowboat or a canoe.

You can find ways to relate to text even if you haven't experienced it exactly as it is written. In fact, because the audience will be receiving your intentional information through their own perspective and experience, it is sometimes impossible to know how your intentions will be received. But if you are direct and sincere, you will likely be successful in communicating.

# Putting Technique into Action

At this point in the course, you've spent more than 20 lessons building your skill and stamina to support communication through singing. Now it's time to apply everything you've learned and put it into action.

Technique is the mechanism through which we communicate. Technique itself has nothing to say. Think of your technical skills as tools. Now it is time to create something that you desire to communicate. Your impulse to communicate moves through your technique and emerges as song. Coordinating technique and communication is critical for effective performance.

This lesson's song is "Danny Boy." The origins of the song are mysterious. In *"Danny Boy": The Legend of the Beloved Irish Ballad*, author Malachy McCourt says:

> Officially, "Danny Boy" is a song of two verses totaling 155 words. Speculation about the meaning of these words is as ripe as when the song was first published in 1913, a year before World War I broke out in Europe.

There are two main mysteries surrounding this famous song:

- *Who wrote the melody?*

The tune is known as "Londonderry Air" and has been used with many different texts. McCourt's book contains fascinating opinions and legends, but in the end, the author concludes that there is no way to know the true composer of the tune.

- *Who is addressing Danny in the song?*

Frederick Edward Weatherly, a British lawyer, wrote the text in 1910 for a different tune. His sister-in-law introduced him to the Londonderry tune in 1912, and "Danny Boy" was rebirthed as we know it today. McCourt again concludes that there is no way to know exactly what voice Weatherly intended for the writer of what appears to be a letter written by a father to his son on the battlefield. However, McCourt points out that Weatherly intentionally composed texts that could be sung by any gender. McCourt presents an argument that by looking at Weatherly's other work, it is likely that the letter to Danny was intended to be from Danny's mother.

As long as you bring your unique experiences and you are intentional, your delivery will be successful in moving others.

Be sure you've completed your character analysis for this piece. Have you made your decisions about where to breathe? Have you identified places that might be tricky vocally and require more practice? Then, using the technical skills you've learned throughout this course, work through the first verse of "Danny Boy" with your fully informed intention, finding your own way to connect to the text.

Oh, Danny boy, the pipes, the pipes are calling
From glen to glen and down the mountainside.
The summer's gone, and all the flowers falling;
'Tis you, 'tis you must go and I must 'bide.

But come ye back when summer's in the meadow
Or when the valley's hushed and white with snow.
I will be here in sunshine or in shadow;
Oh, Danny boy, oh Danny boy, I love you so!

# Danny Boy

Music based on "Londonderry Air"
Lyrics by Frederic Weatherly

Arranged by
Dave & Peg Dunbar

**Larghetto**

1. Oh, Dan-ny boy, the pipes, the pipes are cal-ling from glen to glen and down the moun-tain-side. The sum-mer's gone, and all the flow-ers fal-lin'; 'tis you, 'tis you must go, and I must 'bide. But come ye come, and all the flow'rs are dy-in', if I am dead, as dead I well may be. Ye'll come and find the place where I am ly-in'; and kneel and say an "A-ve" there for me. And I shall

© Arranged 2019 for The Great Courses by Dave & Peg Dunbar.

"Danny Boy" [page 2]

# LESSON 24

# Singing's Surprising Benefits

**FEATURED SONG**

"If Music Be the Food of Love"

**EQUIPMENT NEEDED FOR VIDEO EXERCISES**

none

**LIST OF VIDEO EXERCISES**

none

Singing has benefits far beyond those we can calculate or measure. Music can be healing both internally for the singer and externally for those who experience the singing and music.

*All of us are connected to singing and song. There are very few humans who don't engage with singing and music regularly. Can you imagine a great movie without a soundtrack, a wedding without song, driving with no radio access, or even one day without hearing or humming a tune?*

## How Singing Supports Overall Health

Scientific research has shown that singing has health benefits. There have been studies that suggest that singing improves respiratory and cardiac health, boosts the immune system, reduces stress, and improves mood.

Remember, you are a singing athlete. The simple act of physically paying attention to and working on coordination of posture and breath leads to physical health benefits. There is a focused energy and physicality to singing that brings together physical and mental health.

Singing gives your organs an internal massage, keeping everything flexible and encouraging blood flow. Every time you take a deep inhalation, the diaphragm massages everything below it. As you exhale with singing, sound vibrations move through your body, healing and energizing your mind, body, and spirit in a holistic way.

Because singing is a left- and right-brain activity, it can be balancing and healthy. Singing is generally a right-brained activity, while speech is generally left-brained. By singing text, it stands to reason that we are coordinating and equalizing our brain hemispheres as we sing.

In addition, the awareness and self-care required to maintain your body as your instrument in its optimum state encourages singers to make good choices for their overall health. Simply knowing that you need to be rested, physically flexible, healthy, and hydrated in order to sing with the most ease and comfort is a great encouragement to take care of yourself.

There are several examples of how the type of maintenance that singers do supports health overall.

What you ingest can affect your singing. Some people report that coffee, lemon, or wheat messes with their singing voice. You just have to pay attention to your own physical cues in order to determine what your triggers are so that you can make decisions about your food preferences before singing.

You'll likely notice that you sing better when you are rested. Getting proper rest might be the most important part of maintaining vocal health. This clearly also has benefits for overall health.

Also, it is important that singers are hydrated so that the vocal cords maintain their mucosal property. Because they know that it is important to be hydrated, most singers are careful about excessive alcohol and caffeine intake due to their cumulative dehydration effect. In addition, many singers are careful to maintain hydration in their environment by using humidifiers and vaporizers. Because hydration is good for our bodies in general, the singer habit of maintaining hydration is great for overall health, especially your skin!

Especially for classical singing, it is helpful for the nasal passages to be free of gunk and ready to vibrate. You can use a neti pot or saline spray to maintain open, clear space in the nasal cavities.

Most singers avoid smoking, as they know it will affect their lung capacity. Again, this is a bonus for overall health.*

## Using the Tools from This Course

This lesson's song is "If Music Be the Food of Love." Sing through the melody, applying everything you've learned in this course. Practice it on your own, paying attention to the areas that you are specifically challenged by and giving those areas attention.

Think about how many tools you have! This course is full of tools, and in each lesson you've been given ideas about how to access, develop, and use them. Put these tools in your singer's toolbox and use them when you need them.

Of course, you cannot use all of the tools all of the time. Learning which tools you need at what time is as important as learning how to use them. If you choose a hammer when you need a screwdriver, you might be tempted to be frustrated with the hammer. Watch this temptation as you approach your work as a student of singing. Be cautious of jumping to frustration at your breath when it may actually be a postural issue. When engaging in specific exercises, do your best to remain open and positive to what they might offer you, but beware of overanalyzing or attempting to apply everything at one time!

---

\* Manuel García was a singer, voice teacher, and inventor of the laryngoscope. He was born in 1805 and lived to be more than 100 years old during a time when the average life expectancy was less than half of that. Perhaps his long life had something to do with all of his singing!

Go back through the course and repeat exercises. Consider taking a few private lessons with a voice professional. Don't be surprised if you encounter some of the same things you've learned in this course. You can always use reminders and improvement!

Learning how to sing is a never-ending journey. Because your instrument is adaptable and ever-changing, you can continue to evolve as a singing artist throughout your life.

One of the initial artistic choices you'll have is choosing and programming your own repertoire. Find pieces that speak to you. You'll want to consider your range, tessitura, voice part, and vocal colors as you explore repertoire. Learn what styles you enjoy and what allows your voice to feel free and easy.

This course is designed to support singers of all levels. If you return to lesson 1 and go through the entire series again, you will likely take away different things and continue to improve in your expertise and skill. In fact, now is a great time to listen to some of your recordings from previous lessons—specifically lessons 1 and 2. Compare those sounds to the sounds you are making now. What changes do you notice?

---

**HOMEWORK**

You now have 22 songs that you've practiced and are familiar with. Consider it your final project for this course to schedule a performance. Be creative. You might choose to sing for your friends in your living room or rent a concert hall and hire a pianist. You might choose to perform at a local nursing home, preschool, or hospital. Whatever you choose to do, make it something that's meaningful for you.

# If Music Be the Food of Love
*Sing On!*

Lyrics by William Shakespeare,
dawn pierce, and Dave Dunbar

Music by
Dave Dunbar

© Written 2019 for The Great Courses by Dave Dunbar.

"If Music Be the Food of Love"    [page 2]

"If Music Be the Food of Love"   [page 3]

"If Music Be the Food of Love"   [page 4]

"If Music Be the Food of Love"   [page 5]

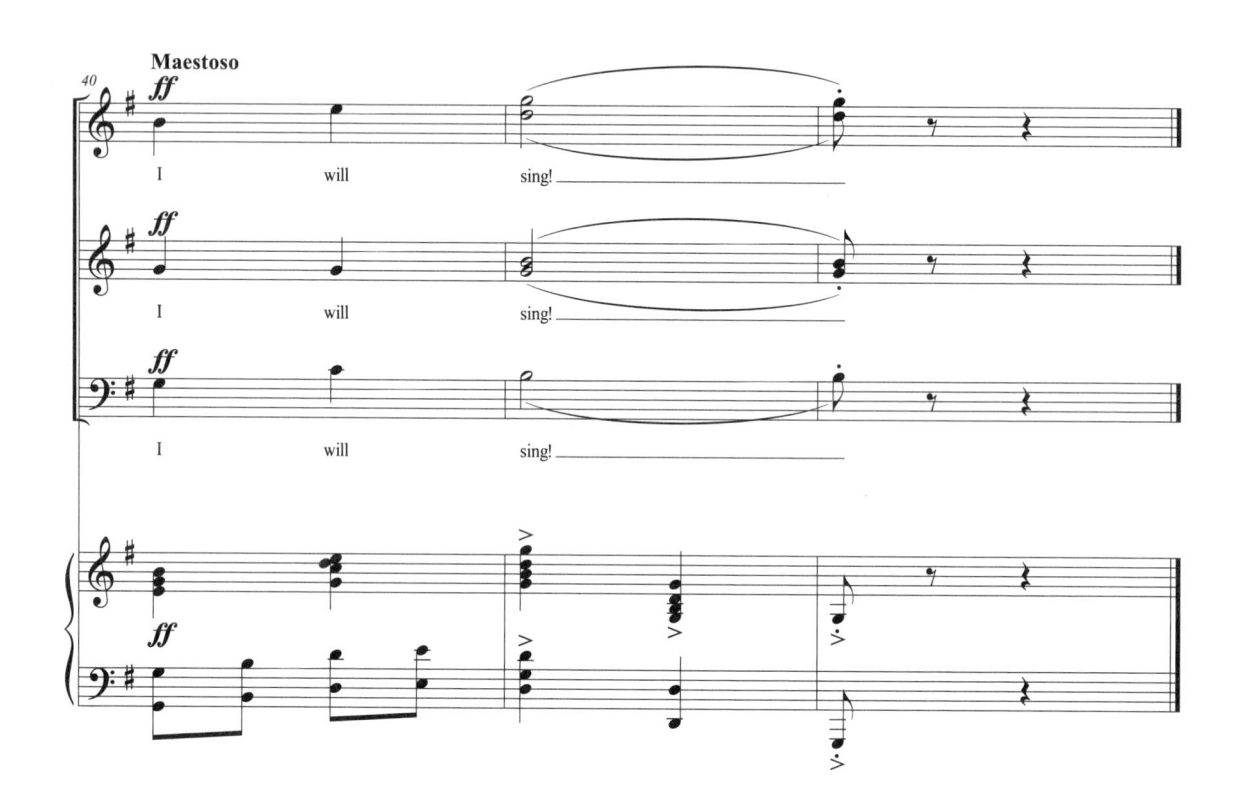

# Glossary

**alto**: Common shortened form of *contralto*; typically refers to the low range of the female voice, typically from F5 above to F3 below middle C (C4).

**appoggio**: Resistance to the chest cavity's collapse on exhale; from Italian, meaning "to lean or to support."

**arpeggio**: A series of notes that forms a broken chord; for example, the first, third, fifth, and sometimes eighth scale degrees of a major chord. For vocalizes, often represented as 1–3–5 or 1–3–5–8.

**articulators**: Parts of the airway used to control the nature of sound passing through the mouth, including the lips, tongue, teeth, and jaw.

**attack**: See **onset**.

**baritone**: The middle range of the male voice, typically from A4 above to A2 below middle C (C4); some baritones may reach C5 above to F2 below C4.

**bass**: The lowest range of the male voice, typically existing entirely below middle C (C4), from E4 to E2, occasionally from G4 to C2.

*Bauchaussenstütz*: Pushing the low belly outward on exhale.

**Bernoulli principle**: In physics, the inverse relationship between flow velocity and pressure; in singing, this principle describes how airflow through the vocal folds can affect the folds' position via a change in air pressure.

**clavicular breath**: Breath that expands the upper portion of the chest.

**complete breath**: Breath that expands the clavicular, thoracic, and diaphragmatic areas of the chest and abdomen.

**consonant**: Vocal sound produced by partially or completely interrupting the motion of the vocal tract.

**contralto**: See **alto**.

**diaphragmatic breath**: Breath that expands the abdomen; a "belly breath."

**Fach**: System of classifying voices not only by tessitura (range) but by multiple qualities, such as tone, weight, and color.

**falsetto**: A "false" register above the singer's modal range, typically extending it upward by about two octaves. Sometimes referred to as a head voice, in contrast to the chest voice of the singer's modal range.

**Garcia position**: A standing posture intended to ensure maximum capacity for inhalation, credited to 19th-century vocal pedagogue Manuel García. In this position, the sternum is raised, intercostal (rib) muscles are expanded, elbows are extended to the side, and hands are overlapped at the small of the back.

**genioglossus**: Muscle that extends the tongue.

**hyoglossus**: Muscle that retracts and depresses the tongue.

**intercostal muscles**: The muscles that lie between the ribs that help to expand or contract the chest cavity.

**international phonetic alphabet (IPA)**: A writing system designed to standardize the representation of sounds among languages; IPA symbols are typically enclosed in square brackets.

**larynx**: An organ that houses the vocal folds and consists mostly of cartilage; commonly known as the voice box or Adam's apple.

**librettist**: Person who writes the words (the libretto) to a long piece of music, such as an opera or musical; from the Italian *libretto*, meaning "little book."

**libretto**: See **librettist**.

**masseter muscle**: Muscle near the cheek and temple that moves the jaw.

**mezzo**: See **mezzo-soprano**.

**mezzo-soprano**: A "half soprano"; the middle range of the female voice, typically from A5 above to A3 below middle C (C4). Operatic mezzo-sopranos may reach from F5 to C3, overlapping with soprano and/or alto.

**neutral jaw**: Jaw position where the temporomandibular joint has released downward but not displaced forward.

**onset**: The type or quality of the first note sung; may be described as breathy, glottal, aspirated, clean, etc.

**passaggio**: A transition point in a singer's tessitura between his or her so-called chest, or modal, voice and his or her so-called head, or high, voice. A singer will struggle to reliably produce the note(s) in their passaggio.

**pitch**: A particular sound frequency; often used synonymously with *note*.

**register**: May be used as a synonym for *vocal range* or *tessitura*, or may refer to a particular portion of a singer's tessitura (i.e., modal register versus falsetto register).

**resonator**: The chamber of a musical instrument in which sound vibrates, as the body of a guitar or case of a piano; in singing, it refers mainly to the mouth and pharynx (upper airway).

**semi-occluded vocal tract (SOVT) exercise**: A category of breathing exercises that limits the amount of air inhaled, often using a straw or other mechanical barrier.

**soft palate**: See **velum**.

**soprano**: The high range of the female voice, typically from A5 to middle C (C4). Operatic sopranos may range from C6 to C4.

**syllabic stress**: The use of pitch, length, and volume to emphasize syllables in a way that affects meaning; for example, the word *recall* with stress on the first syllable means "to call again" or "to call back," whereas *recall* with stress on the second syllable means "to remember."

**temporomandibular joint (TMJ)**: The joint where the lower jaw meets the skull; TMJ dysfunction is a common cause of jaw pain.

**tenor**: The high range of the male voice, typically from C5 above to C3 below middle C (C4), occasionally as far as F5 above and B-flat2 below C4.

**tessitura**: A person's natural, comfortable vocal range. See also **voice type**.

**thoracic breath**: Breath that expands the upper and middle parts of the chest.

**velum**: Area at the back of the roof of the mouth that is soft and pliable; often called the soft palate.

**vocal cords**: See **vocal folds**.

**vocal folds**: The modern term for, and often used interchangeably with, *vocal cords*; two folds of mucus membrane inside the larynx. Passing breath through these folds causes them to vibrate and produces sound.

**vocalize**: A vocal warm-up or vocal exercise.

**voice type**: The classification of voices based on tessitura (range). The most common names for voice types in Western music are soprano, mezzo-soprano, alto (a.k.a. contralto), tenor, baritone, and bass.

**vowel**: Vocal sound produced by free and continuous motion of the vocal tract.

# Bibliography

Adams, David. *A Handbook of Diction for Singers: Italian, German, French*. 2nd ed. New York: Oxford University Press, 2008.

Hearns, Liz Jackson, and Brian Kremer. *The Singing Teacher's Guide to Transgender Voices*. San Diego, CA: Plural Publishing, 2018.

Héritte-Viardot, Louise Pauline Marie. *An Hour of Study: Exercises for the Medium of the Voice*. New York: G. Schirmer, 1880.

Locke, Robert. "5 Reasons Why People Who Sing Are Happier, Healthier and Live Longer (Regardless of How Well They Sing)." *Lifehack*, August 13, 2015. https://www.lifehack.org/293814/5-reasons-why-people-who-sing-are-happier-healthier-and-live-longer-regardless-how-well-they-sing.

Lutgen, B., and Max Spicker. *Vocalises*. New York: G. Schirmer, 1936.

Marchesi, Mathilde. *Bel Canto: A Theoretical and Practical Vocal Method*. Mineola, NY: Dover Publishing, 1970.

Marchesi, Salvatore. *Twenty Elementary and Progressive Vocalises, Opus 15*. Amsterdam, Netherlands: Broekmans & Van Poppel, 1986.

Marzo, Eduardo. *The Art of Vocalization: A Graded and Systematic Series of Vocalises for All Voices, Selected from the Works of Alary, Aprile, Bordese, Bordogni, Brambilla, Concone, Crescentini, Lablache, Lamperti, Marchesi, Nava, Paer, Panofka, Panseron, Savinelli, Sieber, and Others*. Boston: Oliver Ditson, 1907.

McCourt, Malachy. *Danny Boy: The Beloved Irish Ballad*. Philadelphia: Running Press, 2002.

Micu, Alexandru. "Why We Yawn and Why It's Contagious." *ZME Science*, January 10, 2019. https://www.zmescience.com/other/feature-post/yawning-science-contagious-01102019/.

Miller, Richard. *Solutions for Singers: Tools for Performer and Teacher*. New York: Oxford University Press, 2004.

———. *The Structure of Singing: System and Art in Vocal Technique*. New York: Schirmer Books, 1996.

Monahan, Brent Jeffrey. *The Art of Singing: A Compendium of Thoughts on Singing Published between 1777 and 1927*. Metuchen, NJ: Scarecrow Press, 1978.

———. *The Singer's Companion: A Guide to Improving Your Voice and Performance*. Pompton Plains, NJ: Limelight, 2006.

Moriarty, John. *Diction: Italian, Latin, French, German—The Sounds an 81 Exercises for Singing Them*. 6th ed. Boston: E. C. Schirmer Music, 1975.

Paparo, Stephen. "How Gender-Inclusive Is My Choir?" *Alfred Music* (blog). March 18, 2019. https://www.alfred.com/blog/how-gender-inclusive-my-choir/.

Ristad, Eloise. *A Soprano on Her Head: Right-Side-Up Reflections on Life and Other Performances*. Moab, UT: Real People Press, 2002.

Rossini, Gioacchino. *Gorgheggi e solfeggi: Per rendere la voce agile e imparare il bel canto*. Milan, Italy: Ricordi, 1983.

Soniak, Matt. "Why Does Inhaling Helium Make Your Voice Sound Funny?" *Mental Floss*, March 20, 2014. https://www.mentalfloss.com/article/21590/why-does-inhaling-helium-make-your-voice-sound-funny.

Vaccai, Nicola. *Practical Method of Italian Singing*. Edited by John Glenn Paton. Milwaukee, WI: Hal Leonard Corporation, 1986.

"Vocal Tract." *VoiceScienceWorks*. https://www.voicescienceworks.org/vocal-tract.html.

Wall, Joan, Robert Caldwell, Tracy Gavilanes, and Sheila Allen. *Diction for Singers: A Concise Reference for English, Italian, Latin, German, French, and Spanish Pronunciation*. 2nd ed. Redmond, WA: Celumbra, 2009.

"What Is the Strongest Muscle in the Human Body?" *Library of Congress*. https://www.loc.gov/rr/scitech/mysteries/muscles.html.

Zemach-Bersin, David, Kaethe Zemach, and Mark Reese. *Relaxercise: The Easy New Way to Health & Fitness*. San Francisco: HarperSanFrancisco, 1990.

Zemlin, Willard R. *Speech and Hearing Science: Anatomy and Physiology*. Englewood Cliffs, NJ: Prentice-Hall, 1988.

Zi, Nancy. *The Art of Breathing*. Glendale, CA: Vivi, 1997.

## SIGHT-READING RESOURCES

https://www.musictheory.net

https://www.teoria.com/index.php

http://musictheory.pugetsound.edu/mt21c/HarmonicFunction.html

https://tonesavvy.com

https://www.amazon.com/Creative-Approach-Music-Fundamentals-Book/dp/0840029985

## IMAGE CREDITS

**10**: adamkaz/E+/Getty Images; **24**: The Inner Man™ Artwork Compilation used with permission from Medical Illustrations Company; **107**: RapidEye/iStock / Getty Images Plus; **125**: IPA Chart, http://www.internationalphoneticassociation.org/content/ipa-chart, available under a Creative Commons Attribution-Sharealike 3.0 Unported License. Copyright © 2018 International Phonetic Association; **140**: oversnap/Getty Images; **165**: PHOTOS.com>>/ Getty Images Plus

# NOTES